A DISTURBED PEACE

Selected Writings of an Irish Catholic Homosexual

Brian McNaught

A Dignity Publication

Library of Congress Catalogue Number 81-67627
ISBN 0-940680-00-9

Foreword

Sifting through six years of commentary is a little like rummaging through a trunk full of old clothes. At times, you catch yourself laughing about some of the things you once bought and wore. You can't quite figure out where your head was when you made such an investment. On the other hand, it's amazing how many of the clothes still seem to fit. While a few of the colors are a bit bolder than you now prefer, they are nonetheless stylish and comfortable.

When Dignity President Frank Scheuren asked me to collect the best of my writing for publication, he sent me on a journey into my past. It was a delightful, though sometimes painful, excursion into the history of a young man who has struggled to cope with what it means to be both a homosexual and a disciple of the Gospel of Love. My delight resulted from seeing my growth over the years. My pain came from realizing my failures and in wondering how they have adversely affected the growth of other travelers on the same road.

The edited material assembled in this book represents my honest fears, dreams, frustrations and joys over the last several years. It is my hope that sharing these thoughts will help other gay men and women explore and articulate their own feelings and experience their own basic goodness. In addition, I would love to think that non-gay readers will grow to a better understanding and deeper appreciation of the great similarities between themselves and their gay brothers and sisters who also struggle to live well-integrated and loving lives.

I have not attempted to eliminate seeming contradictions and obvious repetitions in this material because they represent an element of growth. My greatest joy in life is recognizing how much I have changed for the better and how much more growth I have before me. The dates which have been included in the Table of Contents and at the beginning of each article will perhaps enable the reader to better understand and chart that developing process. It is also helpful to know that all of the material, with the exception of "Dear Anita," "The Sad Dilemma of the Gay Catholic" and "Forgiveness," was written for a gay audience.

This book is dedicated to Ray Struble, my intimate partner in life since June of 1976. It is with deep gratitude that I affirm his major role in my continuing creation. His support and caring, his confrontation and candor have enabled me to see more clearly my own goodness and to understand more fully my own experience of a loving God.

Special thanks are extended to my good friends (in alphabetical order) Dr. Sol Gordon of Syracuse University's Institute for Family Research and Education, Sr. Jeannine Gramick, SSND, and Fr. Bob Nugent, SDS, of New Ways Ministry, Fr. Paul Shanley of Boston and my brother Tom for their care and concern in reviewing the contents of this book. I am also grateful to the officers and Board of Directors of Dignity for their enthusiastic support of this project.

Newspapers and magazines from which these materials have been printed include *Alive!*, *The Washington Blade*, *Contact*, *Esplanade*, *Gay News*, *Good Times*, *GPU News*, *High Gear*, *Impact*, *Insight:*, *Metra*, *Metro Gay News*, *Out*, *Update*, the *U.S. Catholic* and the *Witness*. I will always appreciate their willingness and sometimes courage in publishing my work. Likewise, I thank Betty Berzon, Robert Leighton and Celestial Arts for their permission to reprint "Gay and Catholic" from the book *Positively Gay*.

CONTENTS

CONTENTS

ON BEING YOURSELF

Before we can begin to love ourselves, which I believe is crucial for sound mental health and total union with God, we have to root out the negative stereotypes with which we were raised and begin to build positive self-images. Once we have identified ourselves as "gay" and affirmed it as an essential ingredient to our uniqueness, we face the question: "Who else do we tell?" Coming out of the closet is one of the most important steps a gay person can take. It has a big price tag, but for the majority of people it has an even bigger payoff. Yet, it shouldn't be done without a support system. Having come out, we emerge into the so-called "gay community" where we are frequently greeted with a barrage of opinions on what it means to be "truly gay." What we call ourselves, how we dress and the components of our love relationships are considered important, but the real essence of being gay is being who you truly are. There is no secret formula or mode of behavior which makes one person more "gay" than another. Once a person has learned to be himself or herself, it is far easier to delight in the many pluses of being gay.

Dear Anita
Late Night Thoughts of an
Irish Catholic Homosexual
October 1978

I am a 30-year-old Irish Catholic middle child of a family of seven. My father recently retired from the General Motors public relations staff. My mother now enjoys the peace of an empty house. My older brothers and sisters are married with children; my younger brothers and sisters are "searching for the meaning of life."

I had 16 years of parochial education. The nuns considered me a "prince of a boy." I was patrol boy of the year, played high school basketball, was Senior Class President and editor of the Marquette University yearbook. Recently I was named one of the "Outstanding Young Men in America" and was asked by a national magazine to share with others the development of what is considered an intense spirituality.

You and I share the same values, Anita. I too am afraid to walk the streets at night. I abhor pornography and drugs. I detest the rat race, the unemployment, the breakdown of the family, the incidence of illegitimate births and the inability of many school children to read and write. I too take the phone off the hook during the *Walton's*. I too miss *Star Trek*. I too cried during the final segment of *Mary Tyler Moore*. If you didn't know I was a homosexual, you would insist that I be at all your parties because Brian has a "great sense of humor." We would be praying together and playing together and you would pay extra to make sure it was I who babysat your children.

Let me assure you that I know you truly believe that your crusade is God's crusade. I also totally understand your fear, disgust or apprehension about homosexuality. Both of us have been raised since we were little to believe that: 1.)

God condemns homosexuality; 2.) homosexuality is a psychiatric disorder; 3.) male homosexuals hate women and are sexually interested in children. We also learned that male homosexuals wish they were women and lesbians wish they were men.

If all that frightens you, think for a minute what it did to me as I grew up with the secret knowledge that for some unknown reason I was physically attracted to men.

I read the same Bible you read. I heard the same sick jokes you heard. For that reason, I never identified myself as homosexual. I couldn't be, I thought. I have shelves loaded with swimming trophies. I dated throughout high school and college and seriously considered getting married on three occasions. Homosexuals were supposed to be interested in children and I find the very thought abhorrent, and the closest thing to women's apparel I have ever worn was the outfit every Altar Boy wore.

Was I psychologically unbalanced? Well, for several years I thought about entering the seminary or monastery. Every time you apply to a Roman Catholic religious order they screen you by having you examined by a psychiatrist. With each interview I would reveal my homosexual feelings and without exception every psychiatrist told me it wasn't a problem. My only problem, they told me, was living in a hostile world.

Eventually I did enter the monastery but the scenario was similar to the one played out in *The Sound of Music* . . . you know, "always late for chapel but his penitence is real. Always late for everything except for every meal." After a while we concluded together that "Brian's not an asset to the Abbey."

Back at Marquette I was a daily Mass-goer. I read the lessons and led the congregation in song. I was labeled "dormitory Catholic" and "the saint." It didn't bother me. Faith is a way of life. Spirituality is an action verb.

Do you know that I didn't have any sexual encounters until I was 21? Most of the men in my class lost their virginity in high school, some earlier. But the "saint" didn't. It wasn't until he "experimented" with another lonely, frightened male student who was also a virgin that he knew what all the excitement was about. It was awkward and mechanical for both of us and ended with expressions of gratitude because it was so uncomfortable we both knew we couldn't possibly be *real* homosexuals.

Jim and I both, however, unbeknownst to each other, continued to have male-oriented fantasies. He asked if we might try it again and, being the rational creature that I am, I insisted that I had to have a heterosexual experience before I ever had another one which was homosexual so that I would know whether or not I had unknowingly closed myself off.

The following year, I did have my first heterosexual experience with a wonderfully patient and sensitive woman. Despite my earnest desire to enjoy it, thereby removing myself from a life of secrets, shadows and stereotypes, I could not experience physical pleasure.

Now doctors and the theologians of my Church say I am what is called a "constitutional homosexual" as distinguished from a "transitional homosexual." This means that my sexual orientation was set before I was old enough to know what was going on. They say age three to five. The only memory I have of being five is making beanbag puppets in Tot Lot and vague recollections of splashing around in Allen Goldstein's plastic swimming pool. But, they say; that's when it all occurred. They have conducted all sorts of surveys and tests to determine what causes a person's sexual orientation, not unlike the studies they used to make to figure out why some people are left-handed when the majority of the population is right-handed.

Do you know what they found, Anita? Nothing. Every study contradicted the other. All they know is that 10 percent of the population is exclusively or predominantly homosexual in orientation. That's 22 million Americans.

I mentioned "transitional homosexual." This term describes an individual who is basically heterosexual but who also engages in homosexual behavior when there are no persons of the opposite gender available, such as in prison or the Armed Forces. Once they are out of those circumstances, they revert back to heterosexual behavior.

Human sexuality, in my view, is a beautiful gift, which like all gifts can be and has been abused. It's like your gift of voice. You can use that gift to create beautiful, inspiring songs which uplift people's spirits or you can sing songs which upset people. You can sing upon request or you can force people to hear your singing when they don't feel up to it. You alone determine when and how you are going to use it.

There was a time when it was taught that the sole purpose of human sexuality was procreation of the species. Women were instructed to lie perfectly still and even refrain from enjoying what was happening. The slightest enjoyment was considered sinful.

Today, we say that human sexuality can be procreative but that it doesn't have to be. We rejoice at the wedding of a young or elderly couple who for one reason or another are incapable of having children. We wouldn't think of asking them to refrain from expressing their love to each other without the gift of sexuality. We know by our studies of infants that every human person needs to be held and stroked. We know that without human warmth, an infant can die or become seriously maladjusted.

We also know that sexual expression is a language. It can mean a variety of things, from "I love you," "I need you," "I'm lonely," "I'm hurt," to "I hate you." The most beautiful expression of human sexuality is when it communicates self-less love. The most abhorrent is rape. Between the two there is a whole spectrum of meanings and values.

Secondly, I would dare to say that I have studied and prayed through Scripture with the same excitement and interest as you have. Your God is my God. Your spiritual goal is my spiritual goal. Your hope is my hope. But we both know how easy it is to abuse Scripture. Slave owners used it to justify slavery. Catholics used it to torture and kill

Protestants. Christians continue to use it to condemn Jews. We are weak human beings who frequently look to the Bible for justification of our position, our fears and even our hatred.

Who today pays any attention to Leviticus:11 when they sit down to a lobster dinner or New England Clam Chowder? Who stones the woman caught in adultery as the Bible insists? Who believes that people get married because they can't control their lust? What priest or minister has ever been denied ordination because he or she had a hernia operation, a crooked nose or humped back? Do we burn red dresses? Do we hang St. Paul's hair-cutting specifications in our barber shops and beauty salons? Rather, don't we explain that much of the Bible has to be understood in a cultural context? Anita, you know that the Old Testament Jews prepared their meals the day before the Sabbath because work was absolutely forbidden on the Sabbath. When was the last time any of us fried eggs and bacon on a Saturday night for Sunday brunch?

Why then do we quote Genesis, Leviticus and St. Paul's letters to Romans, Corinthians and Timothy as justification of our belief that God abhors homosexuality? Scripture scholars insist that every one of those passages has been taken out of context. No one understood the concept of "constitutional homosexuality" until 60 years ago. The Jewish writers of the Old Testament and St. Paul in the New had no idea that anyone was homosexual in orientation by nature. They presumed that everyone was heterosexual and that those engaging in homosexual behavior were heterosexuals mimicking pagan rites, which was tantamount to idolatry. These findings are not by closeted homosexuals who seek justification of their lifestyle. The scholars in question have pursued the accurate interpretation in every area of Scripture. What good is the message of God if it is misunderstood?

In your book and in your national campaign you state your opposition to homosexuals teaching in schools. You and I both know that homosexuals have been teaching in classrooms for centuries. You have told the American people that homosexuals want to wear dresses to school. Wearing the clothing of the opposite gender is called transvestism, and while there are some gay men who have and do on occasion wear women's attire, the majority of transvestites are heterosexual males. And yet, given these statistics, no one is suggesting that heterosexual male teachers wish to wear their wives' clothing to math class.

Likewise with your comments about child-molestation. Persons who are sexually interested in children are called pederasts and I am sure you have heard of the studies which show that the overwhelming majority of pederasts are heterosexuals. Usually the case involves a father with his young daughter. Do we take this information from police blotters and then suggest that all heterosexuals are child-molesters? No. That would be absurd. But that's what you are telling the country about homosexuals and many people seem to believe you.

When you say, Anita, that gay civil rights will prompt homosexuals to flaunt their lifestyles, what do you mean? Do you mean that a homosexual teacher, assigned to teach history, will spend class time describing his or her relationship at home? If that is what you are opposed to, I join you in your crusade. A teacher is hired to instruct students in a specific area of learning. But is that what you mean by "flaunting"?

Isn't the whole battle really centered upon your opposition to the gay man or woman affirming himself or herself as being a happy, healthy, normal, country-loving, God-fearing human sexual being? This is what gay people are saying the whole battle is for them. We are simply saying that we are unable to live healthy, productive lives in a society which insists we are sick and sinful people.

Let me make the case more understandable by bringing it closer to home. Let's for the sake of argument say that your 13-year-old son Bob, Jr., has strong homosexual feelings. What does it mean? It means that even if you asked him about it he couldn't or wouldn't talk with you. This would

probably upset you, especially if you knew there was something troubling him that he didn't feel secure enough to share
with his mother. I have watched you closely, Anita, given all
the press coverage, and am impressed with your devotion to
your family. Playing and praying together are essential ingredients in creating a family unit which will be something a
child can look to for support throughout his or her life. My
folks did the same and have reaped a family strength which is
the envy of many of their friends.

But even given that security, Bob, Jr., couldn't and
wouldn't talk with you about his homosexual feelings. He
couldn't because he wouldn't understand them himself. He
would be aware of the fact that while watching television or
looking through books or swimming at the country club he
was inexplicably excited by the sight of a handsome man but
he couldn't put a label on it. Even if he could, he wouldn't
talk with you about it because your love and Bob's love mean
everything in the world to him and he would never say anything which might threaten that.

Therein lies the tragedy of being a homosexual in today's
society. What makes it even worse, is that despite his homosexual feelings, chances are that Bob, Jr., really isn't a
"constitutional" homosexual. Kinsey revealed in his studies
that while close to 10 percent of the total population is
predominantly or exclusively homosexual, 37 percent of the
American male population have homosexual experiences and
50 percent homosexual fantasies. This means that well over
20 percent of those having homosexual experiences are not
actually homosexual by nature. But because we don't talk
about it, because the subject is taboo, they don't know that.

Getting back to Bob, Jr., though, let's presume that he is
homosexual. (You may say this is an absurd argument because you are sure he isn't. My parents would have said the
same thing because I defied every stereotype.) Who is your
son supposed to talk to? He doesn't understand what's
happening to him. At that age, he would probably change if
he could, but he can't. Does he approach your minister? We

know what kind of reception he would get and so does he. Is there a gay teacher at school whom he respects? Probably not. There are undoubtedly gay teachers at his school but they won't admit it for fear of being fired. Bob, Jr., is alone in the world. For year after year he carries this heavy psychological burden. He likes himself and hates himself. He decides to date and probably really enjoys the company of his girl friends, but he just isn't interested in heavy kissing and is incredibly uncomfortable in any situation where that is expected of him. He jokes in the locker room and laughs with his friends about his Mother's comments on "Adam and Bruce" in the Garden of Eden. He calls his classmates who are weak and effeminate "queer." He even roughs one up to prove his masculinity.

Family and friends praise him for his looks and kid him about his being a real "lady-killer." He watches the smiles of pride that you and Bob have on your faces. What a fine man Bob, Jr., is turning out to be. Inside, he is tearing his guts to shreds. "If they only knew. If they only knew."

The scenario is similar in college. His moodiness bothers you a bit at times but you presume that it is the pressures of school and career choices. What actually bothers him is the pedestal he's been put on and the expectation that everyone has of him to eventually settle down with the Breck girl and produce 2.75 healthy children.

If he makes it this far, then he has some major decisions to come to grips with. I say "if" he makes it this far because the chances are good that he will kill himself before he has to choose to hurt you. Suicide is the number one cause of death of young gay people. A bullet to the head ("He was cleaning his gun"); crashing the car into a concrete overpass ("He must have lost control"); an overdose of drugs ("He wasn't that kind of boy. Someone must have forced him"); or he can die emotionally by abandoning his dreams and accepting the sick and sinful label as a lifelong curse.

I was lucky, Anita. After I drank the bottle of paint thinner and consumed the bottle of pills, I changed my mind. I

drove to the hospital and had my stomach pumped. As the
tears rolled down the cheeks of "The Saint," I vowed never
again to live my life based upon the expectations of others.
Given a choice, I felt they would prefer me to be a living
homosexual than a dead question mark. Some people in this
country, as we both know, would prefer I hadn't changed my
mind.
     But not you, Anita. Beneath all of that rhetoric is a basic
belief in God. It was our God that I wanted to go home to
when I drank the paint thinner. I felt like a kid at camp who
couldn't cope with the hostility of the counselors and the
other campers. Every day was a nightmare. If God wasn't
going to come to camp and pick me up, I was going to run
away and explain it all later. I changed my mind when I
decided that I had paid the same price to attend camp as
every other kid and that camp rules prohibited the counselors
from acting like God.
     If the Bob, Jr., of our story never chose to commit sui-
cide, he would have to choose whether or not to marry. If he
marries, he will fantasize about men while having sex with his
wife. (Many of the people I counsel are married men with
several children. They have been able to perform sexually by
pretending that it was another man they were relating to.) If
he chooses not to marry a woman, then he can attempt to be
celibate (a goal which has met with little success) or he can
seek out a companion with whom he wishes to share his life.
     Anita, let's say that Bob, Jr., comes home and finally
and tearfully tells you that he is a homosexual. I heard you
say on CBS's "Who's Who" that if that happened you would
tell your son that you love him. I know that you would. You
would tell him that you love him as much now as you did
before. He continues to cry and tells you and Bob how hard it
has been for him and how he didn't want to hurt you and
how he feels so relieved that you both now know. He has
missed being part of the family and asks if it is OK to tell the
other three children.
     Into the house walks a family friend, who, in the midst

of a conversation begins talking about "queers" making gains in New York City. Bob, Jr., is sitting quietly with you, attempting to refrain from showing any reaction. The conversation continues. "Those faggots want to dress in women's clothing, molest our children, flaunt their homosexuality, etc., etc., etc."

Do you sit and listen quietly? Do you interrupt and change the subject? What is your husband's reaction? When you have your answer, Anita, you will know exactly how my parents and 44 million other parents in this country react when they hear you on television or read your comments about their children in the newspaper.

What is Bob, Jr.'s reaction? Does he begin to water at the eyes? Does he storm out of the house with thoughts of suicide, revenge, hate, disappointment with you, or pride? You know your son. What is his reaction? When you have that answer, Anita, you will know how I felt inside and how 22 million other Americans felt when they watched the results of Dade County, St. Paul, Wichita and Eugene and when they listen to you speak.

I knew that we were going to lose in Dade County et al., because people don't understand what "gay pride" is all about. They mistakenly see it as one more threat to stable American life. But if you and your family experienced the real psychological terror that Bob, Jr., would go through as a homosexual, you would understand what this "gay civil rights movement" is all about.

It is a primal scream, Anita, by millions of people who want to live. It is an angry denunciation of all of the lies which have been heaped upon us for as long as we can remember. It is a pleading to straight society to refrain from forcing us to live in shadows of self-hate. What could be more inhumane?

Gay civil rights are human civil rights. Competent people should not be denied jobs because of what they do as consenting adults in the privacy of their homes. People should not be denied shelter because of inherent feelings they have had since they were children.

If you want to go on a national campaign against any person who molests children; against any person who recruits children; against any person who sexually forces himself or herself upon another; against any person who is not doing what he or she was hired to do, you will have my talents, energy and money behind you. Homosexuals, however, have nothing to fear from such a crusade.

What homosexuals and every other person under the sun fear is being stereotyped. One band instructor who sodomizes boys is no more an indictment of homosexuality than Hitler's hate for the Jews is for all of Germany; the Ku Klux Klan's hatred of blacks is for all Southerners; the Boston Strangler is for all heterosexuals; Sirhan Sirhan is for all Arabs or Joseph McCarthy is for all Catholics. Nor should a gay person affirming himself or herself be construed as "flaunting" any more than black persons affirming their blackness; Christians affirming their faith, or a woman affirming her uniqueness as a woman.

We are all unique, Anita. Each of us is called to develop our unique talents, totally reflecting the wholeness of our being. No one has the right to deny that process unless it truly interferes with the rights of others.

You state that gay civil rights infringes upon your right as a mother to raise your child in a healthy society. But the healthiest society is that which protects people from blind fear of others and guarantees them the right to life, liberty and the pursuit of happiness. To challenge that is to challenge not only the cornerstone of this country which we both claim to love but also the very fiber of our faith which we both claim to follow.

I will join you in prayer tonight, Anita, requesting that those who suffer might be comforted and that those who are comfortable might be disturbed by the suffering of others. ∎

Coming Out — The Price
August 1979

Five years ago, when I "came out" publicly, I was fired by a woman who was my editor and second mother at the Catholic newspaper. One day last week I received in the mail from her a box containing the "stuff" which I had left behind in my desk.

My first impulse was to throw the box away without looking at its contents. Losing my job and all of the security surrounding it was the most painful experience of my life and I wasn't sure I wanted to take the chance of ripping open that wound. Yet, I was curious and feeling brave (Ray was nearby paging through our photo album), so I began shuffling through the random assortment of memorabilia.

At different times, most especially in the beginning, the process was an exciting journey through a time tunnel. My 1974 capsule contained two eight-cent stamps; a trophy I won from the Heart Fund for riding 40 miles in the Cyclethon; a letter from the Selective Service releasing me from any further obligation as a conscientious objector; a copy of my letter to Peter Rodino, chairperson of the House Judiciary Committee, in which I requested Richard Nixon's impeachment; a pile of addressed but unstamped Christmas cards; my Social Security card and Wilma Koslowski's recipe for coffee cake.

There were also copies of columns and articles I had written and several notebooks of half-sentences from my various reporting assignments. (In one such notebook my writing abruptly ends with a long, undirected line of ink which falls off the page. That must be from the time I fell asleep while interviewing the bishop. Thank goodness he didn't notice.)

As I had feared, my journey through the box was also very painful. It started me thinking about the good times I

had at the paper; about the laughs with the friends I had
made in my four years there; about my career and my great
hopes for the future. I thought about how proud my folks
were and how excited my nieces and nephews got when they
saw their names in my column. I thought about Margaret, the
woman who fired me, and how I felt I was a surrogate son to
replace the one my age she lost. I thought about Mildred, the
black woman who used to strike up an old song for me to join
in every time I walked through her typesetting room. I began
to wonder again, as I have so frequently in the last five years,
why it all had to end the way it did.

A couple of days later I met Paul Guilbert. Paul is the
young Rhode Island high school junior who made interna-
tional headlines when it was learned he planned to take his
boyfriend to the school prom.

Before introducing myself, I imagined what kinds of
things must now be happening to Paul. Since his name
became a household word, I imagined Paul was now receiving lots of letters from all over the world. I imagined he was
being asked to speak at rallies, classroom discussions and gay
conferences. I imagined he was suddenly surrounded by
people who would be happy to sleep with him, to discuss the
movement with him or, at the very least, to call him friend. I
wondered how his teenage life had changed and I thought
about the box he might be shuffling through in five years; a
box containing little reminders of where he had been in 1979,
a place to which he could never return.

After hearing from him that he was well and happy,
though he will be changing schools for his senior year, I
offered Paul a big piece of unsolicited advice. "Paul," I said,
"what you did was very important and will undoubtedly
make it that much easier for others to follow. I am sure you
are being inundated with praise and attention and you should
enjoy every minute of it while it lasts. You deserve it. But be
careful. You owe it to yourself to get your education, to
enjoy the rest of high school and college, to build a personal
and professional life of your own. Don't get swallowed up in

the movement. The best contribution you can make is to develop yourself to your full potential and to be happy. Do you know what I'm talking about?"

Paul smiled his 17-year-old smile. Before he had much of a chance to respond, his attention was being sought by another.

Paul Guilbert is a hero today to a lot of people who want to "come out" but are afraid. While most of these people, like Paul, would prefer not to make headlines, they would like to have the courage to ask a person of the same sex to the high school prom or the fraternity barn boozer or the holiday staff party. And there are still a lot of people who would be happy just to "come out" privately to family and friends.

The process of "coming out" is probably never-ending. I thought it was finished when I made it into the *New York Times*, but five years later I still have to make daily decisions about "coming out" while buying flowers, leaving for airplanes and walking in the park. The process begins with self-affirmation, that important first step when we acknowledge our same-sex feelings. When that acknowledgement becomes self-acceptance, we begin to share the information with those people in our life who either need to know or who we want to know.

"Coming out" to family and friends has been shown to be a positive political gesture. In studies conducted among persons voting on gay civil rights, individuals who knew a gay person generally were shown to be far more supportive than those who didn't. Likewise, "coming out" can be a positive step toward sound mental health. However, as much as I would like to see every gay person and bisexual person declare publicly his or her orientation, I think it important we caution the overly anxious about the possible personal ramifications at this time in history.

The more you come out, the greater your freedom. The greater your freedom, the greater the price you pay. After all, "freedom is just another word for nothing left to lose."   ∎

Coming Out — The Payoff
August 1980

Michael, your Mom doesn't believe you're dead. She wants you to know you can come home. If you're gay, it's OK with her. She loves you.

Being gay is no reason for dying. Spread the word: Being gay is a good reason for living. The time has come to totally eliminate death as a dangling modifier of "gay." Why are they so related?

Recent studies have shown that the majority of gay people who die violent deaths are closeted. Further, a considerable number of killers of homosexuals are other closeted homosexuals. Another group of gay people, many of whom are young, commit suicide. Michael totally disappeared. His friends think he's dead. His mother thinks he vanished in order to be gay. That's dying, too.

I tried to commit suicide once because I couldn't deal with being gay. I also considered disappearing so that I could escape a life of expectations. I've never put myself in a position of being killed by a closeted homosexual, but I understand why some people do. Sex with a stranger, they reason, means no one can trace you.

Last night I had dinner with a young guy who inherited $150,000 from a grandparent, but his father, who is executor of the will, refuses to give him the money until he stops all of this "gay foolishness." He walked away from that inheritance and from a $40,000-a-year job in order to begin being a whole person at age 26. Does he have any regrets? He's as poor as a church mouse now and would love to have a steady income but he would never trade his discovery of wholeness for the price tag on the closet door.

The connection between gay deaths and the blossoming gay young man is that many homosexuals die because they fear they can't handle the consequences of coming out. They have heard similar stories of people being disowned and losing their jobs and they decide it is too big a price to pay. Some of those homosexuals end up feeling trapped between their inner selves which are gay (and craving fresh air) and the exterior world which continually rewards them for not being gay. Unable to feel comfortable with either choice, they choose death, the final solution. Others tolerate the lies because they want the security of family and steady employment. However, they are so afraid of discovery that they choose anonymous sex partners off the street and end up a two-paragraph item in the morning newspaper: "Episcopal priest found naked and bound in bedroom, bludgeoned to death by hammer. No known suspects."

Coming out is a subject of great controversy. In a recent editorial in the *Advocate* newspaper, David Goodstein strongly, and I think harshly, attacks gay people in the closet. He seems ready to push people whether or not they are prepared.

In the past, I have said that people must be allowed to come out of the closet at their own pace. While I still believe that, I think the advice needs modifying. It is cruel and dangerous to throw a reluctant non-swimmer into a pool. Likewise, it is totally ineffective to suggest from a distance that they try it "only if they want to." The option, I think, is for the veteran swimmer to stand in the water with arms outstretched and to continually encourage the person at the side to try the water. "It's safe and it's invigorating." Why would anyone who doesn't swim jump into water without hearing why it's worth the experience and without some assurance he or she won't drown?

Michael, if you're alive, I'm in the pool and the water is wonderful! I promise you that I never felt fully alive until I made the plunge. If you're gay, you're a natural swimmer. It's an essential aspect of being Michael.

When I jumped in the water, I lost all of the security I had on dry land. For a while, it was a security I didn't feel I could live without. But here I am — happy, well-integrated, growing in a wonderful relationship, the object of affection of previously frightened family and friends. I don't have much money but I have something money can't buy — integrity. I no longer fear being discovered. I no longer laugh at "fag" jokes. I don't worry about the mail carrier seeing "gay" on a return envelope, the bank clerk seeing "gay" on a check or the readers of the morning newspaper seeing "avowed homosexual" after my name.

More importantly, I have discovered wonderful things about myself. Some people may scoff at the generalizations, but I have witnessed a sensitivity in me and my gay friends that I have not found in most straight men. I have been freed of role playing too. In other words, I can take bows for my cooking, open doors for men and women, check the oil in my car without ever sensing that any of these activities are inappropriate. That's very liberating.

Affirming my homosexuality has enabled me to be the confidant of friends who now feel they can be honest about themselves without fearing judgment. It doesn't matter whether their issue is being fat, impotent, alcoholic or unfaithful. They now feel comfortable laying it out, shedding some tears and knowing that I can plug into their pain.

There's something about coming out which enables you to be authentic in many seemingly unrelated areas of life. That first important step towards "self" takes you out of the clutches of the "world" and its expectations. Your spiritual life, work life and social life become honest. Games are for people who can't be themselves.

If you jump into the pool, you may swallow some water. You may lose your balance and even momentarily be disoriented. That's part of the birthing process. All real growth involves some pain. But here I am, waiting to grab you, wanting to help you take that first stroke.

Don't jump into the pool unless there is a support system of some sort awaiting you. Don't leap from security unless you can be assured your immediate survival is possible. But don't stay on the sidelines too long. The sidelines mean death one way or another.   ∎

Words of Oppression
February 1980

A lesbian friend was visited by an eight-year-old nephew who, like many of his peers today when at a loss for words and attention, would call people "fag." He called his aunt Marilyn and her lover "fags"; he called Ray and me "fags"; he even called his 10-year-old sister a "fag."

"Do you know what that means?" my friend finally snapped.

"No," he said, somewhat shocked.

"It's a nasty term people use when they are talking about homosexuals," she explained, "and I don't like it."

After a while, the word slipped out again. As before, Marilyn stopped what she was doing and confronted the youngster with the fact she found the term offensive. "It's like calling someone a nigger," she said.

On his third and final slip of the day, she slapped his face.

No doubt Bobby had no idea what "fag" meant for sure, even after it was explained. Nor did he know that his aunt and the three other adults in the room were gay. All of his friends called each other fags; by now it was just a habit.

Marilyn's position, however, was that Bobby was a guest in *her* home — a home she took risks to share with her lover and which at that moment was the scene of a small gathering with gay friends. She didn't care to spend the next couple of hours, not to mention the next couple of days, wincing every time the one syllable slur left his lips. Nor do I blame her.

Fag seems to be an "in" term among even a lot of gay people today. So too is dyke. The people who use those terms are sometimes people who think of themselves as liberated, proud and politically sophisticated. If you ask them about the terms they say, "Oh, 'fag' isn't offensive to me. The word *belongs* to me. I have defused it by adopting it. Now straights can't oppress me with it. Fags and dykes unite!"

Not me, thanks.

Other terms which seem to be "in" among some circles of gay and lesbian folk are found in a poster available through *GPU News* in Milwaukee. It's called "The Language of Oppression" and includes: Fairy, queer, sissy, queen, auntie, flit, swish, Mary, fruit, lezzie and bitch, among others. Surely you have heard the terms; we all have: "Hi, Mary — don't you look ravishing tonight. Who's the queen with you?"

If the opportunity presents itself, ask about the terms. "What, 'queen'? — oh, we're all queens. I'm a queen; you're a queen; we're all just a bunch of dizzy queens. Now don't go getting uppity, sweetheart — you're no better than the rest of us."

That's the crux of it, isn't it? When it comes right down to it, a lot of gay people believe that no one who is homosexual is any more than an old queen or a bulldyke.

Again, no thanks.

Language betrays bias, regardless of who is speaking. Labels, even when accompanied by laughter, are self-fulfilling prophecies. If you call yourself a queen, it becomes you.

Do you remember how funny we thought it was when black folks started calling each other "nigger"? They thought it was funny too. That's why they said they did it. I don't think it's funny any more and neither do a lot of black leaders. It's no funnier than watching a person seek the approval of a group by saying, "Don't mind me, I'm just a Polack!" . . . or "a girl!" . . . or "a sissy!"

About words, John Milton said, "Apt words have power to assuage the tumults of a troubled mind and are as balm to festered wounds." It would seem the opposite is also true. Inappropriate words have the power to stir up the troubled mind and salt the festered wound.

Despite the fact I came out publicly as a "happy and healthy" homosexual five years ago and have read as much as

I could on the subject since; despite the fact I have attempted to work through all of the negative images I was given of what it means to be a homosexual and have tried to help others do the same, I am still working hard at feeling really good about myself and am still battling against those daily doses of negative reinforcement.

I am just now beginning to feel comfortable sensing that aspect of my being which is masculine. I am just now beginning to understand my relationship to God and to the rest of the world. I am just now getting over the emotional shock of watching my world fall apart when I affirmed my gayness before straight society. I don't need to be called a dizzy queen by my gay brothers and sisters. I don't need to hear myself referred to by terms used by others in my past to create a troubled mind and festered wounds. Those wounds are just now beginning to heal.

I am a homosexual male. I call myself "gay" because I find the term is a positive statement about me at this point in my life. It is a term which I helped to create, unlike those created by heterosexuals which have been heaped upon me without my consent. Perhaps tomorrow I will no longer need the word "gay" nor feel it is politically important, for it too can be in the language of oppression.

I am not a man who wants to be a woman. I am a man who wants to discover the full meaning of being human, male and female. Right now I am concentrating on experiencing my masculinity because for so long it has been denied me.

I am not a dizzy queen, though at one time in my life I probably acted a little dizzy. I am not a fairy, faggot, fruit, queer or sissy. Those terms were created by ignorant people who didn't understand me. I need to educate them so that those terms are no longer used to describe homosexuals. They need to know the terms don't describe me and are offensive, regardless of who is using them. ∎

Whose Gay Apparel?
January 1978

Remember when you were a youngster and one of your friends called you to the side of the garage to tell you a "dirty joke"? In retrospect they seem pretty dumb, but at the time most of them didn't make any sense at all. Nonetheless, we giggled and blushed and refused to admit we didn't know what it all meant.

Last night we attended a dinner party which had gathered together a variety of our gay friends. All of us could be described as mature professionals, yet the evening's conversation was dominated by an unending series of sexual puns and innuendo. Suddenly I was back at the side of the garage amidst a stream of giggles and feigned blushes. No one dared admit he or she found the evening predictable but I would guess that most of the people left the party somewhat bored and feeling empty.

As much as I enjoy being gay and as boring as I find most heterosexual cocktail conversation, I am growing tired of the many little accents which have been accepted as essential ingredients to being a homosexual. What's more, I am beginning to believe that much of our humor, gestures and actions betray a subconscious affirmation of the idea that there is something a little queer about being gay.

Given our tremendous ability as human beings to acclimate to any situation, most of us are probably unaware that we are acting any differently than we did prior to our "coming out." Yet, the experience of listening to persons who . are just getting their feet wet prompts immediate reflections of the nightmare we all encountered when we first stepped foot into a gay bar or picked up our first gay publication. While I was filled with a wonderful sense of relief that there were other gay people in the world who didn't fit the common stereotype of homosexual, I was incredibly threatened and insecure.

We hear a lot of rhetoric today by some gay spokespersons that individuals who are concerned about what society thinks of us are "Uncle Toms" and perpetuators of oppression. The attitude presented is that there is a "straight society" and a "gay society" and the distinctions must be preserved. Personally, I find that mentality to be counterproductive. Surely there are areas of common ground among gay men and lesbians which offer us an immediate sense of camaraderie, but there is only one society to which we all belong. I remember back in 1968 when the National Black Economic Development Conference (NBEDC) demanded large sums of money from "white society" so they could establish five black states in the South. Our "white society" was told by our "black society" to ignore the demands because the majority of blacks did not want to live separately. Nor do I.

I do not believe that open relationships, having recreational sex with all of your friends, penis jokes, camp, handbags and pierced ears are the greatest contributions gay people can make to civilization. I have no problem with anyone else engaging in or adopting those items or behavior as their own but I resent the force with which many of them are heaped upon gay people who are just coming out as essential ingredients for being a truly liberated homosexual. Our well-publicized message must be that being gay means being yourself. That means that if you prefer baggy pants to skin-tight jeans or monogamous relationships to open relationships, that's your business. Our message must be that the greatest offering gay men and lesbians are making to society is our ability to be ourselves, our real selves, despite pressure from all sides to conform to some contrived role, be it the role forced upon us by the Anita Bryants of this country or the roles encouraged by some separatists.

Ultimately, being gay means feeling good about your sexual orientation toward persons of the same gender. Being a liberated human being means making your own choices as to how you wish to spend your time, money and energies; how you wish to direct your life; what you wish to hold sacred and what you wish to consider foolish.

If giggling every time someone in the room says, "Come now" is a natural thing for you, do it, but please don't be offended if I don't.   ∎

More Pluses
April 1978

A speaking engagement in Canada necessitated my flying to Montreal in the overwhelming company of a large group of boisterous, beer-bellied, middle-aged, Boston Irish hockey fanatics. Before the Delta flight was 20 minutes in the air, I was already beginning to make mental apologies for being both Irish and a resident of Boston. My only saving grace was being gay. Straight camp has no comparison.

Too frequently, lesbians and gay men find it necessary to apologize to straight friends for some of the idiosyncrasies which are associated with being homosexual. This is not to say that I enjoy being on a plane when the cabin is filled with outrageously campy gay men. I am merely saying that every charge which is made against gay people can be made with equal cogency against the non-gay.

Is there a popular magazine today which contains ads any less exploitative than those in gay publications? Is having a Colt model on the front cover of *Mandate* any more sexist than using Cheryl Tiegs to sell *Time* magazine? Is the alleged narcissism of the gay scene any different than that ritualized by John Travolta in front of his bedroom mirror in *Saturday Night Fever*?

Are Gay Pride Parades any more "offensive" than the promenade on St Patrick's Day in New York and Boston? Are gay motorcycle clubs any more caricatured than the Shriners? Is Edith Bunker any better a representation of the "perfect woman" than the stereotypical "butch dyke"?

While I was in Canada, one woman commented that we spend too much time talking about what is wrong with the gay scene and not enough time accenting what is good about it. What is "good" and "bad" obviously is a matter of opinion, but I think she is right.

Gay people seem far more concerned about exploitation

than non-gays if people are able to believe what they read in
newspapers. Many gay publications deal daily with the threat
of going under because they refuse to accept ads which are
sexist.

Gay people who insist upon maintaining ties with their
religious institutions provide us with the finest examples in
modern history of martyrs for the faith. Who, besides
lesbians and gay men are attempting to get into Churches
today?

Gay people tend to be far less sexist in language, attitudes and actions. As many complaints as we hear about bars
which require women to have three pieces of I.D., there is a
far greater effort on the part of gay men to eliminate language
which defines all people under the category of "man." How
frequently do we see the word "person" substituted in
straight publications for the word "man" or "men" when the
gender is unknown?

Gay people, as a whole, challenge the psychiatric profes-
sion as no other group of Americans has dared before by
ignoring their "scientific" findings, thereby calling into question their credentials.

Gay people are pioneering in the area of relationships
and sexual expression. With no or few role models to follow,
lesbians and gay men have been forced to abandon preconceived notions of the meaning of relationship and by trial
and error have discovered that the healthiest relationship is
designed by the individuals involved.

Gay people are challenging definitions of what it means
to be male and female. We are, again, discovering for ourselves what potential we have for doing things previously
taboo for our genders.

By standing in defiance of near-universal condemnation
and by surviving centuries of planned purges, lesbians and
gay men offer other oppressed persons the hope of becoming
their own persons.

To those persons who are victimized for sexual practices
other than homosexual or heterosexual, the gay movement

has offered a place where fears can be verbalized and hopes expressed. Bisexuals, transsexuals and transvestites are generally greeted with far more empathy than they would ever encounter in straight society.

While it goes without saying that there is much wrong with the general attitude toward the aged, blacks, the handicapped and all other persons who are externally different than the majority of gay people, none of these biases are peculiar to us. Moreover, an objective look suggests, I think, that we are struggling to eliminate the biases and prejudices we each picked up as children from the heterosexual media.

Sometimes it amazes me that any of us even survive the constant pressure we receive from non-gays and from each other. Too often we take our survival for granted as if it was a matter of luck.

This column is not an invitation to end our struggle to eliminate sexism, exploitation, agism, racism, classism, and all of the other evils which plague us as Americans but more to encourage an occasional pat on the back that we have come as far as we have.

More than any other generation of homosexuals in the history of the world, we have the opportunity to make things a lot easier for those who follow us. More than the opportunity, we have the responsibility. Few persons will be aware of our struggle 50 years from now any more than we can imagine life without electricity. But the simple knowledge that the little ones who grow up knowing they're gay won't be forced to hide their light under a bushel should be enough cause for celebration today. Perhaps our liberation will have its effect upon non-gays too so that young straight children will not have to be embarrassed by their parents while accompanying them to a hockey game in Montreal. ∎

The Next Step
November 1980

A woman appearing on a morning talk show recently was introduced as a transsexual priest. She sat comfortably as the host probed into her past but finally concluded she didn't know why she was appearing on his show. The comment, at first, seemed terribly naive. Surely she was there to make people comfortable with transgender identity. What's more, she's the perfect person to test the Catholic Church's ban on ordaining women to the priesthood. But she didn't say that.

Later, I realized what a terrific statement she was making by not needing to make any statement at all. While she said she was indeed concerned about women's rights and the needs of other transsexuals, she wasn't on television to prove anything to anybody. She had hoped she was invited to discuss her study of reincarnation.

What a beautiful message: She liked herself. While her story is fascinating, her statement is profound. This woman is comfortable with herself and doesn't plan to spend the rest of her life explaining her transsexualism.

I would like to think that is the next evolutionary step for gay men and women: that rather than spend our lives defending ourselves to family, friends and working cohorts, we get about the business of being ourselves, enjoying life and putting our homosexuality into proper perspective.

It is an albatross around the neck of most minority people that we feel we must constantly prove ourselves. We stand before the viewing majority and insist through a variety of ways that we are just as reliable, just as decent, just as patriotic, just as religious, just as masculine and feminine, just as normal.

In years past, I, as a white person, have watched black friends straighten their hair, struggle with word pronunciation different than their own and worship in a style which for them lacked meaning. As a man, I have painfully witnessed women friends reject help on the highway, scoff at an opened door and refuse a warm smile. As a Christian, I have been torn by news of Jews feeling the need to change their last names or assemble Christmas lights securely around their front doors. Being a homosexual, I too have felt the need to project an image. I am careful to refrain from public displays of affection, from leaving *Blueboys* in sight of visiting relatives, from being the least bit "effeminate" in front of straight audiences. I have friends who mess up the bed in the guest room so the maid won't know they're gay; who are afraid to subscribe to a gay publication for fear of what the mail carrier might think; who have moved across the country so their family will never know of their activities and friends.

In other words, many of us are living our lives to prove we are or we're not what even strangers might imagine; strangers who probably couldn't care less. I don't think it's healthy.

I don't want my black friends to be white. I don't want my women friends to be men. I don't want my Jewish friends to be Christian. Their uniqueness is part of what I find attractive. If their differences make me uncomfortable, it's my responsibility to adjust. Why then am I so hard on myself when it comes to my differences? Why am I so preoccupied with my homosexuality and the effect it might have on others?

Sometimes I wonder how much of my life is an attempt to prove to my folks that they didn't fail. How much of my life is an attempt to prove to the Church that I am still worthy of its praise? How much of what I do for a living is an attempt to prove to myself that I'm OK?

I want to be freed up of the need to prove anything to anybody. I want to live without expectations and images. I want to let go of the "shoulds" and begin focussing on the "wants and needs."

What does it require to make such a significant evolutionary step? What does the process of letting go demand of us? In the November issue of *Psychology Today* there is a good article about the need to be perfect and the toll it takes. Troubled personal relationships, impaired health, low self-esteem and depression are the potential results of attempting to be something you cannot be, according to the author. We gay people who attempt to be perfectly gay or perfectly straight in the world invite anxiety and exhaustion.

Modified for our purposes, the advice given to perfectionists seems most appropriate. We are encouraged to begin by making a list of all the advantages and disadvantages of living to meet other people's expectations. Where's the payoff? Second, we should determine how much satisfaction we think we will get by playing a role and then play the role to see how much satisfaction we actually received. Another technique is to keep track during the day with a list of the times we compromised ourselves. Why did we do it and what were the results? Eventually, the perfectionist or the person who lives a role will let go of expectations and learn that being average or being yourself is far more comfortable.

That's what I want to be: An average guy who happens to be gay, and, like the woman who happens to be a transsexual priest, feel I have nothing to prove.   ■

GROWING UP GAY

A good friend once commented that the most awful thing about being gay is forgetting how awful it *was*. Too frequently, once we have come out and established for ourselves a comfortable niche, we forget the pain we felt as an isolated person in school and in the family. This process puts us out of touch with those young gay people who follow us in time. It can also prompt us to sever important ties with our families. The support and love of family, both that of birth and that of "adoption," through the coming out process are important to full integration. While the term "Gay Community" has been challenged as a misnomer, we are indeed a family and, as such, have a responsibility to each other. Young gay people need to know they will be supported when they come out. Older gay people need to know they won't be left alone when they seemingly have nothing more to offer. Perhaps the greatest underscoring of the gay family in recent history was in Washington, D.C., in October, 1979, when 100,000 gay men and lesbians from across the United States gathered to affirm their common bonds. "We are everywhere," they chanted, "and we shall be free."

The Prom
June 1980

High school junior and senior proms across the country this Spring were undoubtedly dominated by the scene of tuxedoed halfbacks mockingly tapping the shoulders of their male buddies to ask for a dance. That's alright, guys. Have your fun. Laughter helps ease anxiety. But there is history being made and you're part of it. The rights of gay people have taken a giant leap forward and I couldn't be happier. A U.S. District Court in Rhode Island recently ruled that to deny permission to an 18-year-old senior to take a male escort to the school prom would be a violation of the student's constitutional right of free association. With blackened eye and undoubtedly an upset stomach, Aaron Fricke took Paul Guilbert to the Cumberland, Rhode Island, High School senior prom. Fricke wasn't the first to attend a school prom as a male-escorted gay student, but he was the first to have the support of the courts.

Last year at this time, when Paul Guilbert was denied permission by the same school to attend the event with a male date, I wished out loud for the day when I could chaperone a school prom at which gay couples danced with as much abandon as their straight classmates. Like a parent who endured the Depression, I want those who follow my generation to have more than we did and to be spared unnecessary suffering. The thought of gay high school students being affirmed enough to identify themselves as gay; the thought of them being able to ask a person of their choice to a school function, to be free of the pressure to lie and conform, to laugh at the ignorance of the rest of the world, makes my heart dance.

Were I liberated enough at 18 to ask a male date to my prom and were the world liberated enough to permit it, I think I would have dared to ask Peter Murray to be my date.

Peter was the most handsome man I had ever seen. A transfer student, he had the nicest smile, best body and hairiest chest in school. I don't know that he was gay. I didn't even know that anyone was homosexual besides me and even that I couldn't verbalize. But if I had the chance to do it over again, Aaron and Paul having broken the ice, I would probably ask Peter.

Like every gay person I know, I went to the prom with a "friend." Her name was Martha Bloom. She was a girl with a great sense of humor whom I dated through most of high school. We laughed a lot.

As was the tradition, I borrowed Dad's car for the occasion. I spent lots of money renting a white tuxedo and buying Martha's gardenia. Martha, too, spent lots of money. She bought an expensive gown and had her hair done. She looked great and beamed with excitement over dinner and at the country club. For Martha, this was the magic night to which she had looked forward since she entered high school. The senior prom — the most romantic event in a young woman's life: fancy new dress, orchestra music; no curfew. Her mind swam with expectations.

Martha closed her eyes as we danced. I stretched my neck to watch Peter. Wasn't he handsome? Didn't he look sharp? I wonder if he's having a good time?

I didn't fantasize dancing with Peter. Such a thought was beyond my imagination. I thought more about how I wished we were sitting at the same table and going to the same after-party. I thought how I wished we were close friends, buddies, back-slapping chums.

As the evening drew to a close, I watched the different couples dance slower and closer, slower and closer. The women began running their fingers up and down their dates' backs. The guys nestled their noses into the napes of the girls' necks and tenderly kissed them. Martha held me tight and stroked my back. I cracked a joke and made her laugh. Laughter helps ease anxiety.

That was yesterday. Today is different. Fourteen years

later two men in Cumberland, Rhode Island, danced together at their school's senior prom. The price they paid (and will continue to pay) was enormous. They undoubtedly spent the night keeping each other laughing. They may not have had any fun. But they went and the American judicial system said they had the right to go. Senior proms will never be the same again.

That was today. Tomorrow will be different. Tomorrow young gay men and women will decide if they want to go to the prom. If they do, they will select the partner of their choice. If they rent a tux or buy a gown, they will do so with excitement. They won't need to stare with pain across the dance floor. They won't have to laugh their way through the last song.

Thank you, Aaron. Thank you, Paul.   ▪

Class Reunion
May 1980

The invitation to the 10th anniversary of my college gradua-
tion was signed "Fondly, Charlene." The woman I nearly
married now lives with her family on Pelican Lane in Wis-
consin.

My dark side imagined Pelican Lane being dominated by
turquoise houses on postage stamp lots adorned with pink
flamingoes and shrines to Mary. A subsequent letter from
Charlene was printed on note paper which depicted her
100-year-old farm on five acres of Pelican Lane. It carried a
snapshot of two adorable children and her handsome husband, a former fraternity brother whom I secretly hoped had
gained 200 pounds per year since we left Marquette.

I wrote back that I would love to come to the reunion
were it not for the expense of travel. I lied. At this point in
my development, I don't want to return to my past; I'm not
ready. I feel I have come too far to return to the place where I
protested against all of society's injustices except my own.
Returning to Milwaukee to see the men and women with
whom I shared four significant years of my life would be an
unnecessary confrontation with the unresolved pain of my
experiences there. The invitation alone has already begun the
process.

Some gay people have told me they breezed through college. It was a dream, they say. They went to bars; they were
"out." A few even state they had a lover for a roommate! Not
me. For me and for a lot of others it was a nightmare. Too
often, I think, we gay people who survived the nightmare
and who have built ourselves a happy and fulfilling life allow
ourselves to forget how dreadful the past has been. In so
doing, we cut ourselves off from the pain which continues in
the lives of those who followed us into high school, the army
or college.

At a 10-year reunion I know I would encounter straight peers who would laughingly reminisce about their terror of failing Mark Highland's ethics class or about the time they broke curfew and were grounded during the basketball championships. But I would want to talk about how many times I thought of ending my life because of the "monster" that was growing inside. I would want to talk about how alone I felt in the midst of their laughter.

I remember my college years as an ordeal rather than an opportunity. That's not to say I didn't have fun in college. It was at Marquette that I learned to drink beer and to stay up all night playing bridge. But as was true for most gay men and women I know, college was more significantly a frightening and insecure time dominated by self-hate, pretending and paranoic reacting.

Were I to return to Milwaukee, I fear I would be confronted with the memories of a Brian I barely recognize; a Brian whose anguish continues to anger me and whose awkwardness I have tried to forget. Held securely in the memory of others, he was a man the women murmured was "unattainable." Intensely religious, highly energetic, anxious to please, he was a puzzle unsolved even by himself. His sophomore year he cooperated in the purging of the fraternity pledgemaster who was accused of being "queer." As a junior he fumbled through a homosexual encounter in the dorm and spent the next two years dreaming about the man at night and avoiding him during the day. As a senior, with only one such experience under his belt, he achieved peace by promising he would never sleep with a man he liked.

That's my history at Marquette and while I'm curious if Pat ever got a job, Pam ever confronted her mother and Paulette ever straightened out John, my need at a reunion would be to pull people into the past and confront them with my unresolved anguish. Only then would the women know why I never kissed them at the door like the other boys did; why one day I would propose marriage and the next announce I was entering the monastery; why my moods changed faster than Al Maguire could get thrown out of a basketball game. If they could see and understand that, then I would be able to laugh about the time we staged a food strike.

As is probably true for many people, there are at least two of me in history. There is the Brian who wore the costume and the one who ripped it off. There is the Brian who made noises to distract attention and the one who now wants to talk about being gay. There is the Brian who met others' expectations and the Brian who struggles with his own. I don't understand why I had to go through those painful experiences but I don't hate the other Brian any more than the butterfly hates the caterpillar.

Today, however, instead of investing my energies attempting to reconcile the differences for those "who knew me when," I prefer to spend my time working to make sure those gay people who follow this generation need not be as alienated by their youth.   ∎

My Family
July 1980

A few eyes swelled with tears at a recent Gay Pride march when the crowd passed a young woman and her father holding the sign: "All American Lesbian and Her Dad for Gay Rights." More than one smiling person nudged a friend with a "Look at that!"

I don't imagine Dad and I will ever be holding up such a sign. It's not his style. But he isn't beyond calling Anita Bryant a "horse's ass" nor in saying he feels my participation in the Movement is "important." Mom wouldn't hold a sign either but she does end all her letters to me with "Our love to Ray." There is special affection for my lover in my family. My younger brother even introduces him as his "brother-in-law."

The support goes beyond the immediate family, too. At cousin Patty's fancy garden wedding, she insisted the photographer take a picture of all the cousins and "cousins-in-laws." The large group gathered, took assigned positions and readied themselves with a big "cheese." "Wait a minute," insisted the bride, "where's Ray?" He was in the bathroom. "We have to wait for Ray," she and the others declared. The photographer waited, the cousins waited and a number of very befuddled guests whispered, "Who's Ray?"

In a recent Gallup poll, 80 percent of those interviewed said the family is the most important part of their life or one of the most important parts. Gay men and women comprise at least a representative number of that group. In fact, for many gay people, reconciliation with family is an important step towards self-acceptance.

Without my family, I would be less whole. Without their love and support, I would be less happy being gay. Like other gay people from close families, I find strength in my past and draw courage from knowing there is a small army of McNaught relatives around the country who love me as an openly gay person.

It hasn't always been so ideal. Six years ago, when I came out publicly, there was enormous tension between me and my immediate family and little communication with other relatives. Dad made it clear that if I were to appear on a certain television program, I was never to return home. Mom called my apartment several times and just cried. Sisters and brothers vanished.

My self affirmation as a homosexual caused them great confusion and embarrassment. Though dialogue was strained, gradually each family member let me know how my "new" life was affecting theirs. The folks quit going to church. My older brother got into a fight with his boss who made a crack. Even my youngest sister protested that all the publicity would discourage boys from asking her out. "My life is ruined," she is quoted as saying. They were all hurt and they felt betrayed.

How do you get from such a point of alienation and hostility to a space where the folks are now asking for extra copies of my articles to send to their friends, and my younger sister calls from college because she needs a good quote for her term paper on homosexuality? Was it just a matter of time? No, but it does require time for all healing to take place. Was it because they loved me so much? Love is surely essential but just love is not enough. Actually, the transition required a variety of factors.

Primarily, we gay people who come out to family and who wish to maintain intimate ties need to love ourselves, do our homework, be patient and trust the love of our families. We can't expect parents to be supportive of us as gay people if we communicate we are not happy being gay. If we don't love ourselves as homosexuals, how can we hope others will? Likewise, we can't expect Mom, Dad and the kids to know anything positive about homosexuality. Like most of the world, they only have negative stereotypes with which to work. When we come out, they're going to have questions and we need to be able to answer them. That is why we must do our homework. Being gay doesn't make you an authority on homosexuality.

Mom wanted to know if I was going to hell and I had to be able to answer her in a language she could understand and trust. If I couldn't answer her, I needed to know a source which could. My older sister wanted to know if she caused my being gay. "Remember the time . . .," she would say and proceed to recall an event from our past. With her, too, I had to alleviate guilt by providing accurate information. You don't have to be a theologian or psychiatrist to answer these basic questions. You merely need to do some basic reading.

Your parents need to do some reading also. I gave my folks Laura Hobson's *Consenting Adult*, a novel about a family coming to grips with a gay son. They trusted Hobson's objectivity and found her story very helpful. Also highly recommended are: *Loving Someone Gay* by Don Clark, *Now That You Know—What Every Parent Should Know About Homosexuality* by Betty Fairchild, and *A Family Matter: A Parent's Guide to Homosexuality* by Charles Silverstein.

Patience is the next step. It takes time for people to learn new information and to change their expectations. Patience for me meant answering the same questions from time to time; not confronting the family with displays of affection they couldn't yet handle, understanding that silence doesn't necessarily mean anything other than "I'm confused."

If there was love there to begin with, if the family celebrated a certain special closeness, it will endure. With time, my family learned I was still the same Brian. I still loved to sing. I still cracked jokes. I still figured a way to get out of doing the dishes. If anything, my coming out enhanced my relationship with my family.

Some people feel we shouldn't waste our energy on our families, especially if they haven't responded affirmatively to our being gay. I suspect that many of those people have never found family to be an important part of their lives. Mine, however, is a treasure and worth every nurturing effort. Even though the folks might not march, there have been times when gay friends have watched me interact with my family, poked each other with a smile and said "Look at that!"   ■

Our Family
May 1975

Greatuncle Frank wears thick glasses now to compensate for his cataracts. His thinning hair is rooted in a scaling scalp which has edged its way towards his eyebrows.

Thick skin covers his jagged bones. Purplish veins design his forehead and legs.

A six-pack of beer and carton of cigarettes are his best friends now, although he is friendly with everyone in the nursing home. An unopened Christmas package from two years back adorns his bedside table. Clean underwear waits patiently in his bureau to be used.

At 76, Greatuncle Frank appears to be one of those lost souls who has just barely made it through life and now waits for death's merciful call. As he never married, he waits alone.

But Mother says it wasn't always that way. She says she remembers well when Frank was the hottest thing to hit Detroit. There was no dance contest he wouldn't enter — and win. There was no distance he wouldn't drive for a good time with his many friends.

It seems that in his prime he was quite the mover . . . sharp dresser, smooth talker, fast stepper, and blessed to boot with incredible good looks.

But things changed; they always do. Older and younger sisters had to begin taking care of Frank. Oh, there was nothing medically wrong with him. He just slowed down and didn't really know what to do with himself, once the dressing room lights burned out.

Then the sisters began dying. One by one they went. And Frank was alone.

What greater fear has a gay person than to be a Greatuncle Frank? More terrifying than arrest, more nightmarish than public exposure, growing old and growing alone petrifies a culture based on youth, good looks and an abundance of action.

But why the fear?

All living things grow old. Scientists can't tell us why. They say they can follow the growth and regeneration of cells and understand the process until it stops. Then, for no reason yet discovered, the body cells quit regenerating themselves and the person begins showing signs of what we call aging. Hair whitens. Skin loosens. Bones become brittle.

It will happen to all of us. Today's Greek beauty is tomorrow's old man. There's no stopping it, short of an early death, so it is something we might as well reconcile ourselves to — or change our distorted value system.

But is the greatest fear being wrinkled or being alone? Are they synonymous? And if so, why?

Recently I read the comments of one grey gay writer who suggested that older gay men are more oppressed by the gay community than by straight society. Laughter and snide comments behind the back greet older gays who dare to presume they are welcome in the bars. The writer suggested that the only thing the culture looks for from older gays is money — and connections.

Elaine Noble asserted in Provincetown, Mass., recently that straight society doesn't have to worry about the gay movement. The gay movement will kill itself off with its own infighting.

Until the gay community begins to consider itself a family, we're going nowhere. Until we quit knocking each other out of the scene because of age, appearance, dress, sex, race, handicap, religion, political stance, marital status or purity of sexual orientation, we are going to continue to be "that sick minority" which hides in dark places, regardless of what the Psychiatric Association says.

If we, who have something to gain, don't show concern for each other, who will? If we, who are gay, don't begin to create alternative lifestyles for ourselves, who will?

Before being gay, we are all persons with human needs. We seek, like all other humans, to have those physical, emotional and spiritual needs met in the company of people with whom we share common ground. Being oppressed for being affectionately attracted to persons of the same gender is a very strong common ground.

How have we met the needs of our brothers and sisters? We stand silent while others receive chemicals and electric shocks. We stand silent while others commit suicide. We stand silent when another is fired, arrested or abused for being gay.

We sneer at women. We sneer at blacks. We sneer at Catholics. We laugh at the handicapped, the unattractive and the elderly.

Welcome to the family.

Concern for the gay community cannot end with the last call for drinks. Leaving the bar is not leaving the problems, for being gay has much more to it than being in heat over someone of the same sex.

Being gay means sharing a legacy of oppression. It means sharing the experience of growing up with a "secret"; sharing the fear of being discovered; sharing the excitement of a relationship; sharing the scourge of the Church; sharing the silence of friends; sharing the prospect of growing old alone.

Being a family means reaching out to, loving and caring for even those we are physically, emotionally, politically or spiritually uncomfortable with. It also means searching for life's positive values and applying them to a community or persons with whom we share pain.

Being a family does not mean feeling obligated to have sex with anyone who enters the arena. Nor does it mean not being attracted to the physically beautiful. But it does mean seeing beauty in each human being and being open to verbal intercourse.

Every one of us will eventually face the poor vision, thinning hair and sagging skin of old age like Greatuncle Frank. But none of us should have to do it feeling the solitary confinement and rejection of our pre-family days.   ∎

The March
December 1979

Since moving to Boston, I have walked Jeremy, my Irish
setter, around the same path each day, and from time to time
have spotted a handsome young guy clipping lawns and
hedges. Sometimes he would smile at me with interest, but
generally he would make eye contact and then look away
shyly. "He's gay," I decided. "He's probably 15, gay, and
doesn't know how to deal with it." I wrestled with what
approach I should take. Remembering how isolated and
frightened I felt in high school, I wondered if I shouldn't
introduce myself and subtly reveal my sexual orientation.
Then he would have someone with whom he could share his
secret. Yet, would I be introducing myself if he weren't
attractive? Maybe I shouldn't start something. Besides, what
if he's straight? What if he's a homophobe? I have to live in
this neighborhood. Better keep walking.

Finally, after three-and-a-half years, we spoke our first
words. "What's the dog's name?" he asked, looking up from
his weeding. "Jeremy," I responded, feeling an embarrassed
rush. "Nice dog." "Thanks." "See you later." "Yeah, see you
later." After a few more of these brilliant exchanges, we
learned each other's names. "His name is Caleb," I told Ray.
"He's a senior in college — older than we thought — but I still
think he's gay." Perhaps next Spring I'll ask him. Yard work
is finished for the year.

"Brian," I heard an excited voice shout as I was marching
with about 100,000 other gay men and lesbians down the
streets of Washington, D.C. "Brian," I heard over the laughing and cheering and singing and chanting and clapping. "I
knew you were a homosexual!" screamed the familiar figure
who made his way through the crowd. "Caleb!" I exclaimed.
"I knew you were gay too." Then from behind me came a
chorus of "Hi, Caleb!" from the large contingent carrying the

banner of one of Boston's most popular bars. So much for the
"isolated and frightened" theory.

A bit later in the day, as I was looking out from the
speaker's platform upon the jubilant sea of gay humanity
which stretched in powerful waves to the base of the Washington Monument, I spotted a ruggedly handsome, mus-
tached man waving and smiling at me from the front ripple of
spectators. I waved and smiled back. Another brother
intoxicated by the spirit of the moment, I thought. At the end
of the presentation, however, the young man was awaiting
me behind the platform, his hand still waving, his smile still
glowing. As my body swelled with that all too familiar
sensation of guilty excitement, I strained my eyes to see more
clearly. "FRANK," I gasped. "I can't believe it." It was my
younger brother's best friend from high school, whom I
hadn't seen in ten years. We kissed and hugged and exchanged quick stories between our cheers for the bold dec-
larations of independence which were resounding from the
stage. "If you're ever in New York . . ." he insisted as he
walked backwards into the mass. "I promise . . ."

Caleb and Frank are only two of the many familiar faces
spotted in the parade and rally which brought together a
mighty army of lovers from throughout North America.
They are only two of the many thousands of stories which
are being told and retold to friends back home who ask
marchers, "What was it like?"

It was like nothing I had ever been a part of before. It
was magic. It was spiritual. It was energizing. Though clouds
threatened us throughout the day, I remember it as bright
and nippy. The sky was aglow with multi-colored flags, pla-
cards and banners which proclaimed the good news of being
gay — of being gay and from San Francisco; of being gay and
from Atlanta; of being gay and from New Mexico, Alaska,
Oklahoma, Michigan and Missouri; of being gay and religious; gay and atheist; gay and black, white, red, yellow,
brown; gay and young; gay and old; gay and proud; gay and
alive, gay and whole. "We are everywhere," we chanted as

we marched to the beat of kazoos and tambourines. "We are everywhere," we screamed as we danced and skated and skipped like children. We embraced each other with shiny-faced grins of excitement. We renewed each other with winks and squeezes and outstretched arms. "We are everywhere," we insisted, "and we will be free."

Funny thing. I didn't want to go to the march. I was upset by the reports I was getting about the planning process and the division it was causing among community leaders. I felt blackmailed into coming. I thought that I had to be there for the mere sake of body count. I wish that my friends across the country who didn't come had been there. They too would have been delighted. They too would have been healed by the day of unity we experienced. That's not to say there weren't things we can't improve upon next time. And there will be a next time.

Next time I want to be one of 500,000. Next time I want to walk through the crowd and see the faces of my high school basketball coach, the lifeguard at the pool and my fraternity pledgemaster. I want to be able to throw my arms around the Brother who taught me English senior year, and to kiss the guy who after school used to watch "Adventures in Paradise" with me. Hell, I want to kiss Gardner McKay! I want to see more nuns and more GIs and more grandparents. Next time I want to see a bishop hold up his half of the sign which reads, "We are Everywhere."

Incidentally, the minister who lives down the street has a son who might be there. I think he's 16 and feeling isolated. ∎

FRIENDS & LOVERS

Like their heterosexual peers, most gay men and women seek to share their love in relationships of mutual respect and support. Having been isolated from each other from the very beginning, having been denied the important growth process of dating and courtship with a person of their own choosing, having to live in a world which promises to punish them for affirming their homosexuality, the majority of gay people find it very difficult to meet new friends, to build a healthy love relationship and to make it last. Family, Church and society generally are unreceptive. Likewise, homosexual men and women even find little encouragement for their relationships from some of their friends. It is a heroic task to commit yourself in love to another when all advertising, gay and straight, encourages you to pamper your every whim. Nonetheless, people who discover that sex and physical attraction are generally low on the list of priorities of successful love relationships are succeeding.

Meeting New People
September 1980

The most pressing question for the gay people I meet is not
how to survive in a hostile world but how to meet other gay
people. How do you make friends and how do you find a
lover?

We have been systematically isolated from each other
for fear of what acknowledging our homosexual feelings
would mean to us socially. When we finally do dare to acknowledge our nature and go looking for mutual support, we
generally enter a subculture of bars which continue to isolate
us. God bless the bars for being a place to gather but I know
people who have frequented the same watering holes for 10
years and have yet to establish a significant friendship. They
have slept with plenty of people but have never had a stimu-
lating conversation with another gay person. The tragedy of
this is most glaring when someone from the bar community is
murdered and the morning paper quotes unidentified bar
patrons as saying, "I saw him frequently but I don't know
anything about him."

Part of the problem is with the environment of many of
the bars. The loud music and dim lights discourage conversation. Part of the problem is with society and the penalties it
enforces for being gay. Many gay bar patrons still fear public
exposure if they tell too much about themselves to the person
on the next stool. However, most of the problem, I feel, falls
on the shoulders of the individual and his or her expectations
of what will be found in the bar.

While there are some exceptions, the majority of people I
know who frequent gay bars are in an endless search for Mr.
or Ms. Right. And if they aren't searching for the perfect
person, they're generally in pursuit of the perfect orgasm.
What we all probably know in our hearts but fail to acknowledge is that there is no perfect person awaiting our arrival and

that no orgasm has much significance outside of a relationship. Each person is flawed in some way but has the potential to be a wonderful friend and lover. Sexual experiences outside of a relationship are like a whiff of poppers or a toke of grass. They frequently provide momentary pleasure but generally are only a distraction from the real need to love and be loved.

Relationships of love and support with other gay people, I think, are essential to our happiness. (Lovers are basically friends with whom we choose to share our lives in a more intimate way.) But all relationships begin with risk. We risk that we will be rejected. We risk that we will have our investment of time and energy wasted. We risk being hurt. But we also risk being loved, accepted, supported and embraced and that makes the risk worthwhile.

When do you take that risk? Significant relationships are made possible when the two people share some common ground. Too often in the bar scene that common ground is simply that both people are gay and both find the other physically attractive. Experience suggests that's not enough upon which to build a friendship. Much of our desire to bed down an attractive person is based on our own feelings of inadequacy. If we can get that "hunk" to take an interest in us, we reason, we must be OK. Even in these situations, many potential friendships end after the first sexual encounter because one or the other is less than totally satisfied with the sex they shared. They didn't talk to each other so they don't know what common ground they share. Further, they fail to acknowledge that few people experience great sex the first time with another person. Sex is like a pair of new shoes. It is frequently only with time that it becomes comfortable and fully satisfying.

I don't think good looks or a nice body belong at the top of a person's checklist of desirable traits in a future friend or lover. (It's nice to be in a relationship with a handsome person but it's funny how good looking the person you love becomes with time.) In fact, appearance might be No. 21 in this list of 20 things my friend Sol Gordon looks for in a friend.

"People I like," writes the well-known sex educator, "have a sense of humor; have a passionate interest in something; have high energy levels; are tolerant of my changing moods; know how to listen; are creative; enjoy touching; are enthusiastic; exude self-confidence; appreciate my successes and are sympathetic when I fail; appreciate when we can be together and don't fuss when we are not; have a sense of justice and injustice; are sensitive to the needs of others; can take risks; have an air of mystery about them; are not sure of everything; are optimistic; don't make fun of people; can offer love unselfishly; are people in whose presence I like myself more."

Your list may vary but the point is that we all have things we look for in other people. When deciding whether or not to risk ourselves in a potential relationship, we need to know if we share significant common ground with the other person. What is even more important is our own determination to be the kind of friend and lover to others we hope to have them be to us.

But how do you meet these people? In every city which has an identifiable gay community there are political, religious and social organizations. (If you are unaware of these, they are listed in the local gay newspaper or can be found by getting a copy of *Gayellow Pages* from Renaissance House, Box 292, Village Station, New York, NY 10014. Tell them where you live and they will send you the complete guide to gay-oriented organizations, bars, periodicals, etc., in your section of the country.)

The people who join these organizations are looking for the same sort of support system we all seek. While you may not be enthusiastic about their political stance, religious views or their social activities, you are not committing yourself to them by attending one meeting. You are merely putting yourself in a setting where you may have your first meaningful conversation with another gay person.

While conversation in the bars is more difficult, it is not impossible. Before opening your mouth, it's important to remember that everyone who surrounds you is equally shy, equally nervous and equally hungry to make friends. The tough exterior of some is their way of pretending they are mean and macho. That's supposed to be sexy. If you don't talk to them, they, like yourself, will undoubtedly go home frustrated, lonely and feeling a little stupid about the charade.

Pick out the people in the room who look as if they are most being themselves. Walk over, smile, stick out your hand, say, "Hi. I'm just looking to make friends tonight. My name is . . ." If your gesture is rejected, the other person will probably kick himself or herself in the morning. At least you tried. The alternative to trying is living a frenzied life among people who will say, "I saw him frequently but I don't know anything about him." ∎

Making It Last
February 1977

It was Winnie the Pooh — his adorable pudgy arms out-stretched in a futile attempt to capture a delicately beautiful butterfly. "Oh Pooh, how I do love you!" the inscription read. "To John, with love, from Brian, Valentine's Day, 1971."

It was my finest offering, representing hours of drawing and precise blending of pastel water colors. When it was finished, it was ceremoniously placed on a dining room table — an "altar" surrounded by flickering candles, uncorked bottle of burgundy and two goblets. There it and I waited anxiously for John's arrival from work.

But like Pooh's efforts to capture the butterfly, the wait was in vain. John didn't come home from work. He preferred, instead, to be with someone else. It was Valentine's Day — the celebration of erotic love, and I sat frustratedly alone.

It was this dashing of expectations which led me into my first gay bar, where I ceremoniously bought drinks for the house. "Happy Valentine's Day from Brian."

In retrospect, the memory is overflowing with humor. My bar bill was moderate, given the fact that it was only 8:30 p.m. (How was I to know that no one really arrives until a fashionable 11 p.m.?) But at the time, it was a nightmare of an evening. I plied myself with gin and tonics, screaming inside for relief from disappointment. As a hopeless romantic, struggling to believe that gay love was no different than straight, Valentine's Day represented every hope for a happy, fulfilled future. I watched that hope being regurgitated into a wastepaper basket next to the livingroom couch where I deigned to suffer my fate and greeted the morning with a resolution to end my life and all the pain which accompanied it.

Eight years have passed — eight years, three relationships, a hundred probings with couples and individuals seeking counseling and a thousand conversations with gays from Bangor, Maine, to San Diego, California. After all of that time, all of that listening and speaking, all of that reading, digesting and regurgitating, all of that love gained and love lost, I understand far more Pooh and his futile effort to capture the "elusive butterfly of love."

Valentine's Day, the commercialized celebration of hearts, flowers and "love means not having to say you're sorry," should have far more significance for gay men and women than our annual celebration of the Stonewall Revolt and the birth of gay liberation, for it is our inability to come to grips with love which cripples us as a people more than our inability to proclaim on national television that we are "avowed homosexuals."

The pursuit of love is the most basic common denominator to all persons, be they male or female, gay, straight or bisexual, black, white, yellow, brown or red, one-year-old or 140. Love is an absolute which defies difference. The sooner we gay men and women accept that, the sooner we will liberate ourselves to experience its richness.

As a person who has been invited to speak to and hear from assemblies of gay and straight individuals across the country, I have encountered the position on love from radical feminist separatist to Roman Catholic Cardinal. I have heard defenses of open relationships, monogamous relationships, auto-relationships, group relationships and no relationships. Modeling my earthly wondering and wandering on a Siddhartha-like trek, I have abandoned all preconceived notions, experimented with new ideas, espoused an openness to all expression and maintained a policy of non-judgment.

I have heard, believed and enunciated that gay people are different than straight: gay expression of love, because it is outside cultural expectation, is more honest and liberating; we are pioneers in the area of relationship and our greatest offering to civilization is the beauty of sexual freedom.

Bunk!

Likewise, I have heard that gay men and women are pro-
miscuous; unstable; unable to satisfy a sexual hunger.
Again, bunk!

While it is true that the isolation gay persons are forced
into during the "Wonder Years" prompts a certain behavior
and while it is true that the lack of societal encouragements
such as tax benefits, religious ceremonies and peer pressure
can make stable relationships more difficult to maintain, gay
men and women ultimately seek the same stability and fidelity, the same richness of love non-gay persons seek.

Maintaining a firm commitment to refrain from offering
to anyone absolute criteria of judgment, I nevertheless
offer here a hypothesis which has proved personally en-
riching.

Experience, observation and the "voice within" insist
upon a belief in pure love being approached as an absolute
which permeates the existence of all things living and dead
("dead" is not the proper word but is used to describe those
things — plants, animals and persons — whose earthly forms
have deteriorated). That love is called God, soul, life and a
variety of other terms. Our ultimate goal as persons inside
and outside the human form is to experience the perfection of
love. Just as experiencing the perfectly developed body
requires hard work and pain, so too does experiencing perfect
love.

Love, though One entity, is multifaceted and is expressed in a variety of stages. There is the love that a mother has
for her child, which is based upon a dependency. There is
brotherly love (or sisterly love) which culturally has never
called for sexual expression. And there is erotic love — the
love of Valentine's Day, the love of sexual partners, the love
which brings people together into relationship.

A primary stage of erotic love is physical attraction —
nice placement of chest hair, nice breasts, nice face, nice . . .,
etc. That progresses into being attracted to the person's mind,
the person's sensitivity to people — the deeper, more
aesthetic values of personhood.

In erotic love, we attempt to break down the barriers which separate us from the objects of our love. We seek to get to know them better — to have them know all there is to know about us and to learn their uttermost secrets. For us, that is a sign of intimacy — of union. Most of the world we see around us does not go beyond this stage of development. Most see this candid sharing as being the essence of love — its ultimate manifestation.

Once the last morsel of secrecy has been revealed, there is a letting down of enthusiasm. "The magic is gone," as some people describe it. The honeymoon is over. Boredom sets in. The body, which once caused an immediate excitement, has become as familiar as the old painting on the wall which no longer elicits wonder. The personality, which has been completely revealed, shows signs of frailty and failure, inadequacy and shortcoming.

"Why should I spend the rest of my life with this number?" we ask, "when there are so many exciting people out there with whom I could be really happy." We long for the exciting days of discovery again — the days of finally disrobing the body we were only able to fantasize about before. We long for the flowers, the little gift surprises, the intimate dinners over candlelight, the newness of background, family, etc., etc., etc.

And so we break up. We divorce. We move out and on to better horizons. We fear stagnation in our early years and leap back into the race before it is too late to compete.

"The consequence," writes Erich Fromm in his acclaimed *The Art of Loving*, "is one seeks love with a new person, with a new stranger. Again the stranger is transformed into an 'intimate' person, again the experience of falling in love is exhilarating and intense, and again it slowly becomes less and less intense, and ends in the wish for a new conquest, a new love — always with the illusion that the new love will be different from the earlier one. These illusions are greatly helped by the deceptive . . . sexual desire."

The most obvious question is "Why bother?" Why

should I spend the rest of my life with someone who no longer excites me physically (especially when I have a very strong sexual drive and there are so many gorgeous specimens waiting to be discovered); no longer excites me intellectually; no longer fascinates my probing mind nor satisfies my emotional needs?

In fact, argue some, why should I stay with a person who is causing me emotional pain — a person who is being cruel and unloving? I have no desire, they state, to spend the rest of my life with someone I am going to be constantly fighting.

In order to go beyond this critical stage — this period when excitement has waned and boredom set in — there would have to be a mutual understanding of what possibilites lay ahead. What is the carrot which leads us on?

Where are the examples? Most persons can't point to their parents as representations of the fine gifts involved in love's higher levels. Many heterosexual partners who have "stuck it out" did so because of "the children," religious and cultural pressure and the fear of what they would do if they actually did break away. With the softening of sanctions against divorce, more and more persons are declaring their freedom and singing the praises of such a move.

If, historically, those couples had shared the dream and goal of love's ultimate gifts, then I would have to accept their experiences as proof positive that this illusive carrot is a lie. But it hasn't been tested properly and has only been written about in abstract terms. Even the Church, in its naivete and lack of understanding of Christ's real gift, has insisted upon fidelity under pain of serious sin. In this, it has failed.

"To love somebody," states Fromm, "is not just a strong feeling — it is a decision, it is a judgment, it is a promise. If love were only a feeling, there would be no basis for the promise to love each other forever."

Why make such a promise? Because, after love has left the stage of the selfish and emerged into the level of the selfless, the human spirit begins to experience a perception, a unity and an internal peace which is otherwise totally impossible. That perception, that unity and that peace defy description by persons who have not experienced them. All of us, at one time or another, have touched for the briefest instant the perfection of spirit. Abraham Maslow calls those moments our "peak experiences."

Commitment to one individual, while not excluding love for all other individuals, enables us to come face to face, soul to soul, with the dynamic power which unifies all of life. "Erotic love," states Fromm, "if it is love, has one premise. That I love from the essence of my being — and experience the other person in the essence of his or her being. In essence, all human beings are identical. We are all part of One; we are One."

By eliminating the traditional reasons for loving another and going beyond their "lovability," we enter into a cosmic sharing of life-love-God-essence-what have you.

A Zen Buddhist psychotherapist described it to me as a mountain jutting into levels veiled from the city below by a fog. The overwhelming majority of people live at the base of the mountain, totally oblivious to the possibilities of climbing. From the city you can see small fires built on the sides of the mountain, indicating the places where others have dared to climb. The largest gathering of fires is shortly above the city. Like a pyramid of light, they decrease in numbers as the mountain increases in height. The climb up the mountain represents the levels of selflessness. The ultimate experience of letting go brings the individual to an awareness which cannot even be imagined from the valley below.

Jesus spoke in terms of giving sight to the blind. The Pharisees, who had the faculty of sight, were blind, according to Jesus' narrative. His life, which merited Him the designation of divinity, was the ultimate expression of selfless love. As such, He was totally comfortable with all persons and stands out as the historic example of ultimate peace. I have come, He said, so that the blind may see.

We constantly remind ourselves that "gay" is an adjec-

tive and not a noun. The gay person who seeks to experience
ultimate love; who seeks to build his or her fire at the top of
the mountain; who seeks to see, has the same opportunity as
any other person.

My experiences in relationship prompt me to admit that I
could not make such a journey with everyone. One lover,
with whom I spent a couple of years, presented obstacles
over which I don't think we could have come, especially at
that stage of my development. The other would have been a
beautiful traveling companion had we known enough to
share the same vision, thereby enabling us to overcome the
boredom period which everyone encounters.

There are several real-life everyday obstacles which gay
men and women, in particular, have to face. For instance,
most gay people have been locked up for so long that we are
like puppies who insist on sniffing every bush in the park.
While our heterosexual peers were initiated into the rituals of
dating throughout high school and college, we either panto-
mimed or refused to cooperate, thereby being denied the very
essential period of psycho-social development. "Coming out"
threw us into a candy shop where we could finally touch and
feel the bodily warmth of that which before we could only
fantasize. We are in a fetal stage of sexual development.
Hopefully, history will be sensitive to that when describing
our emergence. With the same hope, perhaps all persons who
grow up in this country in the near future will be able to
experience the ritual of dating and courtship at the same age,
despite sexual orientation. (I would love to be a chaperone at
a high school senior prom where gay students danced together with as much excitement and comfort as their straight
classmates.)

In addition, even if an individual is raised in an open and
healthy environment, psychologists and sociologists do not
expect persons to make definite choices about anything until
their early 30's. Dr. Daniel Levinson, professor of psychology
at Yale University, states emphatically that persons between
the ages of 22 and 28 naturally avoid strong commitments,

preferring rather to "hang loose." It is not until an individual passes through the early 30's crisis that he or she begins to make long-lasting commitments to job or relationship. If that is true for non-gay persons, how much more likely and natural it is for gay men and women to refuse to limit their options. Dr. Levinson would argue too that the age with which a gay person felt comfortable making long-lasting decisions would inevitably come later in the 30's, given the obstacles to their developing adulthood.

(A side effect of this analysis is the light it sheds upon the difficulty encountered in relationships between persons separated by years in age. One is naturally prepared to settle down while the other, just as naturally, is not.)

Another element which must be considered in gay relationships is children. "Unless human beings are close to children they have little ability to think about the future," insisted Margaret Mead, internationally renowned anthropologist. Gay people, she stated, should involve themselves in households which are microcosms of all of human life . . . older people, children, women, etc.

How often have we seen or witnessed the emptiness which surrounds a family holiday, such as Thanksgiving or Christmas, when celebrated by individuals without a family. Even the coziest gay couples often find themselves longing for the squeals of a youngster and the teary reminiscences of an oldster.

The extended family offers gay couples the opportunity to satisfy the natural desire to give direction and nourishment to the young and relieves the fear of growing old and disabled alone.

I have, of course, avoided the head-on question of the role sexual freedom has in the personal commitment to one individual. Does emotional fidelity necessitate sexual fidelity? If love of a particular one prompts a universal love of others, what does that say about our sexual expression of that love?

Reserving the proverbial option to change my position, I

believe that sex and love have been foolishly linked as being one and the same. I also believe that we are foolishly preoccupied with the subject of sex. It possesses us and drives us. It has the power to totally control our lives, making it impossible to think clearly.

Persons who have lived long periods of time together testify that sex gets better and better, lending credence to the belief that sex is most wonderful when it is a total expression of selfless love. We have also heard persons argue that their sex has been enriched when they have had the freedom to express themselves outside the home or when they and their beloved are engaged in a "threesome." The question of sex and the role it plays in a person's development and attainment of selflessness is an open issue from my present level of consciousness, but I am comfortable in affirming one guideline: If you are ready to make a permanent commitment to another person, and that person in his or her current stage of development is not able to cope with non-monogamy, don't throw it all away in the name of sexual license. That's like opting for a lifelong wheelchair because your driver's license has been suspended. The opposite is true. If your lover's commitment to sexual freedom is preventing you from committing yourself to making the journey together, relax. The sexual appetite will mature.

While it is entirely possible for everyone to live out his or her human existence jumping from one magical moment to another, never having to face the calling to grow beyond immediate satisfaction of artificial needs, life here and beyond here offers experiences in personal wholeness, unity and peace which are within our reach. To choose the opposite is to take Pooh's fixed place on the page, a constant distance from ever reaching the elusive butterfly.   ∎

Monogamy
February 1978

Why is it that many gay men have as much trouble mentioning the word monogamy with their friends as a closeted homosexual would have with the word "gay" at a Knights of Columbus convention? If you say it over and over again in front of a mirror it doesn't sound dirty at all.

Once upon a time I thought monogamy was the only framework a relationship could have in order to be *legitimate*. That attitude undoubtedly reflected my Irish Catholic background and my paranoia that a lover would leave me if I gave him the chance. But from my reading of popular gay literature and from travelling to a variety of gay conferences, I learned that I was unsophisticated; worse yet, I was "unliberated." Before that time I thought that I would be perfectly happy settling down with someone for the rest of my life, but by talking with some liberated gays I learned that true gay happiness results when you can romp in the hay with anyone you want, whenever you want. Not wanting to be unliberated I went home and proceeded to destroy in my foolishness what was a wonderful relationship. Having secured my freedom, I entered the Garden of Bliss and eagerly approached the Trees of Pleasure. I ate to my heart's content expecting that I would never again hunger. However, after a period of time, I noticed that I was wasting away to the point that I hardly recognized myself.

Soon I encountered another pilgrim who had also followed the siren song into the garden. He too looked a bit emaciated. After a while we decided that we liked each other very much, but it was difficult to see each other clearly because the fragrant and lush leaves of the trees blocked out the light and came between us. So, deciding that we were both hungry for something we couldn't find in the Garden, we took each other's hand and walked out together. Risking the label of "unliberated," we built our own garden.

In agreeing upon monogamy as a fence for our garden, neither of us is suggesting that we don't frequently long to run naked through the Garden of Bliss. Our nocturnal emissions and auto-erotic behavior are often centered around the sights we encountered or imagined we would encounter there. Nor does it mean that we will pick up and leave if one of us breaks down the fence on a lonely day and quickly ducks into the lush foliage. It means merely that we have a shared vision of the kind of garden we would like to build together and experience has taught us that bringing in plants from the other garden will eventually guarantee that ours will be overpowered. We have no desire to break up the plants.

Having an ideal relationship is not unlike having an ideal of the physique you would like to develop or the level of spiritual wholeness you would like to experience. If someone asks you "What will it be like?" you will be unable to answer until you develop it. For the time being, all you have is an idea of what you believe will make your life the best possible experience.

As discipline is required in building a body and establishing an intense level of spiritual awareness, so too is it called for in creating a love relationship. If you wish to develop your body into a beautiful specimen of human form, you begin restricting your diet and your time. You cut back on foods which will contribute to fatty love handles; you turn down invitations to go to the movie on Tuesday night because that's your night to work out at the gym. You strain yourself deliberately because you know that building muscles isn't easy. If it was, everyone would be a Colt model. To develop a strong spiritual base, as is the intention of the Trappist monks, you discipline yourself by going to bed early and rising early. Your day is routinely divided into scheduled sessions of individual and communal prayer. You know that Thomas Merton did not write *Seven Story Mountain* after staying up until 11:30 each night to watch "Flash Gordon" reruns.

Likewise with a relationship. While you don't have the ability to verbalize the exact form or the levels of selfless love you will experience, you know from past practice what contributes to mutual growth and what destroys it. As with everything else, you make sacrifices which aren't easy to make. After three relationships and an extended period of "liberation" in the Garden, my observation is that monogamy is the best road I can follow to achieve what I believe will be an incomparable experience. Monogamy, in this sense, cannot be used as the answer to jealousy and possessiveness. Those are the natural feelings which accompany infatuation, not love. Nor is monogamy the best route for everyone. Not everyone wants to have a beautiful body, given the price, nor does everyone seek to achieve great levels of spiritual awareness given the sacrifices. Perhaps monogamy isn't even necessary to make work what Ray and I hope to achieve in our relationship, but neither of us was able to make it work when we were "liberated" and neither of us wishes to sacrifice this relationship in the effort.

■

Open Relationships
March 1977

When David brings home a trick, John moves into the guest room. The next morning, John looks forward to meeting and talking with the stranger who occupied his bed for the evening.

David has one night out of the week set aside by mutual consent during which it is expected he will go out and not return until morning. Sometimes he will bring home a friend with whom both he and John can relate physically.

Peter and Mark have been living together in San Diego for 11 years. Though they haven't had sex together in ages, they are lovers. Genital gratification is sought outside the home.

In both cases, the two persons who have come together in "relationship" have no doubts they will spend the rest of their lives together. They love each other to the point that they are willing to make a commitment to be a part of each other's joys and sufferings.

Neither couple is presented here as an *ideal* way of maintaining a relationship. But they do help to illustrate a point.

Human intelligence and our sophisticated means of communication have liberated us to establish our own dreams, our own course and our own method of actualizing both in our lives.

Throughout the world and throughout time, individuals have entered into relationship with other individuals for a variety of reasons. We read with astonishment about marriages that were arranged by parents before the children were born. We hear about persons in their 80s and 90s joining in wedlock. We know that the marriage of kings and queens were most often political alliances. While rampaging through the bar, looking for a pretty face, with thoughts of John and

Liv Walton guiding us on, we are bewildered by any arrangement which is inconsistent with our dreams and our life course.

Not only are we bewildered, we are threatened. For some reason, we have an ideal of what a relationship must be in order to be valid. That ideal frequently places sex in the position of primary importance. Some of us insist that sexual fidelity is the most important criterion of love. Others insist sexual freedom is by far the most essential ingredient.

When the person with whom we have entered a primary relationship violates or threatens our position on sex, we more often than not decide to end it all and seek out another person who will adhere to our rules.

John and David and Peter and Mark are criticized for their relationships by those persons who want their own relationships to be monogamous. Why? What is so threatening about the ability of other persons to find happiness in their lives? John and David and Peter and Mark tell me that they feel a peace together they have never felt before. They don't walk the floor at night worrying about whether or not the other person *really* loves them. They don't throw up from the fear that the lover will find someone else who satisfies them more.

If I am threatened by their arrangement because it is working and it is the opposite of what I think the understanding on sex should be, I am not very secure in my ideal, my dream, my life course. Likewise, if a couple who has insisted upon an "open marriage" is threatened by a monogamous relationship which seems to be working, they aren't very secure with their concept of relationship.

What is an *ideal* relationship? It depends upon *your* ideal. Ideals change with growth. Perception must change with discovery. Does that mean our earlier ideals were silly? Not at all. They represented where we were and we have to be true to where we are. Does that mean that when our ideals change we have to change partners? Perhaps, but I would hate to think so. If you and your lover entered your relationship after honestly communicating (the key word) your ideals and if you shared experiences and grew together, chances are that your ideals would change together. If they haven't, they may with time.

A couple who enter an open relationship, for instance, may with time decide they prefer to be monogamous. The opposite is true. And with time, the question of sex will probably be placed in its proper perspective.

If having a consistent sex partner is all relationship is about, it would be smarter to find a young whore. The price of services rendered couldn't possibly match the amount that goes into food, board, gifts, vacations, etc.

If, on the other hand, your ideal relationship is based on deep love; if your dream is to share yourself as a friend and companion with another; if your life course is to grow and discover, be sick and healthy, rich and poor in the company of a particular one whose devotion and whose growth prompt an internal peace, then seek out a person who shares your ideal, and don't settle for less. Sex will take its appropriate place.   ■

Cheap Sex
August 1978

Our allies, the sex educators, are now telling their audiences that a man who has one sexual encounter after another with women doesn't love women, he hates them; for if you love something, they reason, you don't use it carelessly and then discard it. They are saying that "machismo" is another word for *rape*, because one of the apparent trappings of caricatured "masculinity" is dispassionate force. Moreover, they are insisting that the advertisements we see on television, in magazines and on billboards which depict scantily-clad women and men are not sexual, they're anti-sexual.

The basic premise is that sex is not and should never be portrayed as the perpetual pursuit of the multiple, simultaneous orgasm with another "body," but rather, sexuality is the wonderful, fun-filled way we have available to us to express care and concern. Above all, they say, sexual expression demands responsibility.

While gay men and lesbians are certainly going through their own sexual metamorphosis insofar as we are only now beginning to discover from experience and from each other what homosexual love is, we nonetheless share with heterosexuals the same socio-religious and cultural roots and therefore share generally the same attitudes toward sex. Despite our many advances, we also frequently share the same distorted understandings of masculinity and femininity; the same adoration of youth and beauty. Perhaps then, we ought to consider what we are communicating to each other with our advertisements, our language and our mannerisms. Is our message sexual or anti-sexual?

When I hear heterosexuals decry the psychological effects of the "lay 'em and leave 'em" syndrome, I think about the stories I hear from friends who have vacationed on Fire Island or in Provincetown and the frustration they felt when the person they met on the beach got up out of bed after reaching orgasm, showered, dressed and began his search for another encounter. Although my friends knew that they might never again see the people they had sex with during that time, they nevertheless felt cheap, lonely and used. When I hear the sex educators decry machismo, I ponder the growth of leather flight jackets, short hair, mustaches and faded blue jeans in the gay male community and I worry about what is happening to our self-concept. I see fewer smiles and more pocket handkerchiefs in the bars these days and I wonder what it's saying about care and concern.

The "I Like the Box" cigarette advertisements of the straight world certainly have their counterparts in gay publications. It is difficult to find a service for rug cleaning or real estate today in some magazines and newspapers without staring at Jack Wrangler's pectorals. I like Jack Wrangler's pectorals but I feel somehow that someone is attempting to capitalize upon sexual frustrations in order to sell me insurance. Wrangler is presented as a piece of flesh to a buying public, which is allegedly only interested in flesh.

My problem with all of my own examples is that I like to fantasize about one sexual encounter after another with the Colt models. I like machismo and own my own flight jacket, occasional mustache and faded jeans. I enjoy paging through a magazine and seeing one hunky number after another. That's what scares me and confuses me.

Deep down inside I believe that sex is most beautiful when it expresses love, whether it be for the special "other" in one's life or for the many special others in one's life. I know too that being raised in an Irish Catholic environment has done bad things to my concept of sex, self, the world, sin and guilt. Yet, even aware of that, I think that I am being equally manipulated by the "image makers" in the gay community.

The gorgeous bodies which constantly dominate our more popular publications have made 93 percent of the gay men in this country feel inadequate about their own bodies. Now, I made up that statistic but I would bet my collection of

Mandates that I'm right. Even people who have every reason to be proud of their physiques are intimidated by the fantasies of others. What is worse, I would wager that the majority of people who are involved in gay relationships are dissatisfied with the body of their lovers. That's not healthy.

I think we have all been co-opted. Despite our protest that we are unique and that we have something new to say to the world, I think we are responding to heterosexuals like well-trained lab rats. We decry the way they objectify women and put them in the role of sex object, but we turn around and do the same to ourselves. They tell us we are not real men and real women, so we men dress up in all the costumes we have seen in John Wayne movies. They tell us that we are human garbage and we respond by using each other and then throwing each other away.

I think we have something unique to say to heterosexuals about sex and love and mental health, but we seem to be taking more steps backward than we do forward. In honesty, I am, at this moment, less concerned about what gifts we have to offer the world than I am about what the whole process is doing to me as a person. Sometimes it really scares me.   ∎

Life's Real Meaning
February 1981

My 90-year-old Grandmother explained over the bridge table the other night the reason she seemed peculiarly distracted. Tuesday would be her 68th wedding anniversary. Each year since Gramps' death, Gram has spent an unplanned week in reflection on the 60 years they shared. Many of the days are teary. She misses him. On some occasions, though, you can get her laughing by asking her to recall a few of the events in their lives together. On the night of their honeymoon, for instance, the band with which Gramps played clarinet showed up outside of the hotel for a surprise serenade. "Gramps had me stand at the window and wave," she says with a smile and waving gesture, "so that he could sneak out the back door to buy cigars for the boys."

Last night, my partner, Ray, and I saw a film in which a brilliant professor decides to separate from his wife and children because he sees their seven year marriage standing in his way of doing something meaningful with his life. He seeks to know the ultimate truth of existence and feels that his wife, children, dinner parties and household chores are all roadblocks to discovering the true meaning of life.

From time to time, I catch myself looking at Ray and wondering about our spending the next 55 years together. Most of the time, the thought is a delight. Once in a while, though, it frightens me.

It frightens me when I fear I may have made a "mistake." The thought of spending the rest of my life with Ray scares me when I imagine I am possibly being held back from discovering "the real me"; that my potential to write the great American novel or replace Phil Donahue is being sapped by my commitment to Ray and my daily routine of walking and feeding the dog, tending to the canary, listening for the rinse cycle, periodically checking on the spaghetti sauce and watching *Little House on the Prairie*. I fear growing fat rather than wiser. I wonder whether this relationship will enable me to have the best mind, the best soul, the best body, the best income, the best sex, the best time I can have OR would I be my best alone or with someone else?

I suspect those fears put me in the company of a lot of other people, including Ray. Surely, my Grandfather entertained doubts from time to time, too. I think the doubts are a normal part of a developing relationship. Yet, some people, gay and straight, suggest that these doubts are a good reason to avoid making commitments to another. They see them as inevitable. They feel that no one person can totally meet all of your needs, so why limit yourself to one person. Grandma's 60 years of marriage is seen by them as more of a tragedy than a cause for celebration.

Most people today, I believe, enter relationships for primarily the same reasons. We seek intimacy and security. We seek relief of the fear of loneliness. The human experience of love is rooted in human need. We long to be affirmed completely by another person. We long to be understood, cared for, respected. We say we do it for love, but *real* love is the fruit of, not the reason for, entering relationships.

Grandma and Grandpa's first few years, like Ray's and mine, were undoubtedly marked by excitement and enthusiasm. During the period of infatuation, we are blinded to the other's faults and we dream without question of total, unending commitment. We feel "complete." One day, the magic wears off. Boredom leads to demands; demands prompt distance; distance encourages doubt. One or both of the lovers begin to silently and then publicly confront the other's faults. This new honesty is threatening and hurtful. Each responds by encouraging more distance. Soon, the doubts begin to dominate. "Did he really love me all of this time or did he love his image of me?" And, "He's changed. That's not the man I married!" It is at this point that many relationships end in bitterness and frustration.

It is this experience of disappointment, perhaps en-

countered over and over again, which prompts some people
to angrily denounce relationships and to publicly deny their
need for intimacy. Yet, it is fully human to seek intimacy and
some hungry people express that need by an anxious preoccu-
pation with genital encounters.

Of those people who have stayed in relationships after
the end of infatuation, some have done so because of cultural
or religious sanctions, because of a sense of responsibility to
the children or because they were afraid to be alone. Many of
these individuals spend the rest of their lives isolated, angry
and regretting their decision to marry.

Other people, however — and I hope to be one of them
— discover that the new honesty is eventually liberating and
that the true fruits of relationship have yet to be tasted. While
before there was a need to be perfect, now there is the freedom to be yourself and to explore new possibilities. While
before there were demands for joint pleasure, now there is a
realization that both parties are individuals, alone in the
world and responsible for their own happiness. Rather than
continuing to feel attacked by the other's honesty, we grow
to experience their acceptance and affirmation of us as the
flawed persons we all are. Rather than feeling betrayed by
our awareness of the lover's faults, we are energized by our
ability to love maturely all that which is imperfect.

I look forward to the future because I believe that as
Ray's and my relationship grows more mature, I will learn to
confidently celebrate my individuality; that I will be energized to give myself more completely to others; that I will let
go of my need to be in control. When Ray and I first got
together, we described relationship as a means of enabling
each other to grow to our full potential. Somewhere along
the line, like most everyone else, we lost sight of our goal and
began to function as one entity. Mature love encourages individual growth in the presence of one who is patient, forgiving
and supportive. The essence of a mature love relationship is
mutual respect.

At the end of the movie we saw last night, the professor

comes face to face with the soul of existence. The secret, he says, is that there is no secret. The one thing in his life which saves him from meaninglessness is his relationship with his wife. Without love, he discovers he is nothing. Whether or not I write the great American novel or replace Donahue is irrelevant. Successes don't make life successful. I think the essence of life is learning how to love. For me, at this point in my development, that means making a commitment to Ray, walking and feeding the dog, tending to the canary, listening for the rinse cycle, periodically checking on the spaghetti sauce and watching *Little House on the Prairie*. For Grandma, it means continuing to grow independent of Gramps and being occasionally nurtured by thoughts of the 60 years they shared.   ∎

THE CHURCH

Gay men and women who affirm themselves as homosexuals and who also affirm their spiritual or cultural
ties with organized religion are caught in a double bind.
The churches generally reject the participation of
openly-gay people. Likewise, large numbers of vocal
homosexual men and women castigate those who seek
to be included in the worshipping community. Catholics, especially, given the size, influence and authority of
the Church, are battered by both fronts. Some of the
criticism by gay people of those who seek the embrace
of the Church is prompted by what is seen as duplicity.
Some people who see the Bible as a call to arms against
social injustice view religious gay caucuses as do-
nothing social clubs. However, within the ranks of
spiritually-oriented gay people there is an army of
modern day martyrs for the faith who hunger for justice
and suffer indignities for their beliefs.

In Defense of Faith
March 1981

When I was a youngster, many of my friends talked with excitement about what they wanted to be when they grew up. One wanted to be a clown and travel with the circus. Another hoped to be a lawyer like his Dad and make lots of money. For as long as I can remember, I wanted to be a saint. Catholic school children were raised with stories of the great saints in history, like Tarcisius, the young boy who died rather than let his friends discover the Holy Communion under his tunic he was taking to the Christian prisoners; and like Maria Goretti, the young girl who died rather than give up her virginity. The nuns would interrupt class at any time to reverently tell the wide-eyed students about the heroics of individuals whose love for God came before their love of life.

I wanted for nothing more than to be God's best friend. Believing a saint to be a "perfect person," I prayed daily, was obedient to my parents and teachers, never said "damn" or "hell," guarded the refrigerator between noon and 3 p.m. on Good Friday so no one would eat, built elaborate May Altars for the Blessed Mother and said home "Masses" by tying a towel around my neck and passing out Necco wafers to my little sister and brother. I would cry during movies like *The Nun's Story* and *Keys of the Kingdom* and dream about the day I might endure chopsticks being plunged into my ears like the Chinese martyrs rather than give up my belief in God.

God was my secret buddy with whom I had numerous private conversations. "If you help me catch the ball tomorrow on the playground, I promise I will try to avoid 'bad thoughts'." And "If you'll help us beat Notre Dame High I promise I will think again about going into the seminary." I missed the fly ball and Notre Dame won but throughout the years God remained my best friend and confidant.

My Church provided me with a clear definition and

picture of God. For many years, it was appropriate and helpful but as time passed, it lost its validity. I found the academic reasoning of early theologians irrelevant. Nevertheless, when, as a gay man unable to cope with the hostility of the world, I tried to commit suicide, it was to the loving embrace of God that I sought to return. Today, before meals, we and our guests acknowledge the presence of God and give thanks for the good food, good friends and good times we share. Even prior to speaking engagements, I discuss with God the need to use me as an instrument of healing.

Among some circles of fundamentalist Christians, it is pure folly for a homosexual to speak of an affection for and devotion to God. One San Francisco minister, in fact, suggests that all homosexuals be executed, presumably to make the country more God-like. Among some circles of gay men and women, too, admission by another homosexual that he or she believes in God is considered the same as admitting you still have your childhood blanket.

To both groups the message needs to be communicated that large numbers of gay men and women have a special meaning in their lives because of their belief in and experience of God. Like love, the experience of God is individual and unique. Many gay people find their experience of God heightened by their participation in religious gay caucuses and the Metropolitan Community Church. For perhaps even larger numbers, their Faith is privately nurtured in less organized ways.

My understanding of who or what God is certainly is different from that of many Christians and Jews I have met. Moreover, it is different than my understanding of yesterday or the day before. Inasmuch as I have no pictures of God to show or visions, miracles and voices I can document, it would seem much easier to prove God as a figment of my imagination rather than a reality. Yet I believe, as Rosemary Ruether wrote Thomas Merton, that, "only theology bred in the crucible of experience is any good." It is through my experiences of living as a gay male in 20th Century America that God is real.

If I was forced to provide for skeptics a definition, I would say that God, for me, is life itself. God is the positive force in all living things; the unifying element of the universe. I am far more comfortable, however, describing the feelings which accompany my experience of God. St. John said that God is love. When I truly love, I experience that inner peace, security, direction and unity which makes my existence joyful, meaningful and unique. Though the moments are brief, when I am in touch with my own shared divinity I experience clear thinking, deep perception and inner warmth.

I am aware of those sensations when my actions prompt growth in others and when theirs create growth in me. I feel the presence of God when I still the distractions of the day, let go of my expectations and open myself up to listening. The absence of God in my life prompts feelings of emptiness, confusion and despair.

Without doubt, I believe the recognition of God's presence in my life is what enables me to be confident in the midst of turmoil, to be hopeful in the battle against oppressors, to be successful in a relationship of love.

It's not easy pursuing Faith when the Church upon whose lap you learned of God drops you to the floor. It's difficult talking about God in the presence of people who have been scourged by the alleged representatives of God on earth. I am as angry and bitter as anyone about the persecution I and others have felt at the hands of religious institutions, but my Church is not my God and my God need not pay for its sins.

When I was in Fourth Grade, the mother of two of my playmates called to complain to my folks that I was attempting to convert her daughters to Catholicism. I thought I was saving their souls. Today, I have no vested interest in whether or not someone is Catholic, or, for that matter, believes in God. I do have an interest, however, in defending my beliefs, and those of others, against the attack of people who are uncomfortable with the concept of a gay theist. Too many gay people feel pressured to deny this special meaning in their lives because they are told it's impossible or immature. The night I woke up my younger brother to tell him about the Chinese martyrs and the chopsticks I learned about in the Fifth Grade that day, we spent several hours coming up with a list of tortures we didn't think we could endure. (Jerry Falwell wasn't on that list.) Finally, we decided we had better find a hiding place in the event the Red Chinese came marching up our stairs that evening.

Today, it's the Moral Majority and a few outspoken gay people who are leaping up the steps and I'm not hiding. I'm as proud and as comfortable with my Faith as I am with my homosexuality.   ■

The Sad Dilemma
of the Gay Catholic

August 1975

With the black sleeves of his religious habit shoved halfway
up his hairy arms, the small finger of his left hand busily
picking wax out of his ear, Brother made quite clear to the
senior honors religion class what the position of the church is
on homosexuality.

"If you come into my office and tell me that you have
shacked up with some broad," announced the school's senior
guidance counselor, occasionally eyeing the wax on his little
finger, "I'll talk to you. But if you tell me you're queer, I'll
kick you out of the office."

Officially, the position of the Roman Catholic Church is
that the homosexual orientation is in itself not sinful, but the
expression of it is gravely sinful.

Yet, upon admission of his or her orientation, the homosexual is kicked not only out of the guidance office in the
Catholic high school, but out of the pulpit, seminary,
convent, monastery, charismatic prayer group, place of
employment, home, apartment, family and circle of friends.
Homosexuals, upon confession or discovery, are kicked out
of the Christian community until such time as they admit
their illness and seek the cure of a psychiatrist or equally
misguided priest.

Because of its roots and its history, because of its size and
its influence, the Roman Catholic Church is seen by the gay
community as the southern white racist of the black-white
struggle; as the male chauvinist pig of the female-male struggle; as the bullying Teamster of the UFW-Teamster struggle.

With roots in the Jewish tradition, Christians are the
adopted children of sexist bias and sexual taboos — biases

Reprinted with permission from *U.S. Catholic*, published by Claretian Publications,
221 W. Madison, Chicago IL 60606.

and taboos which are unexamined in light of the Law of Love.

Sodom and Gomorrah, Leviticus, St. Paul's Letters to the Romans and Corinthians, seem proof of God's disgust with homosexuals.

But modern Scripture scholars insist Sodom and Gomorrah has nothing to do with homosexuality. The legendary destruction of the cities was brought about by the wickedness and perhaps inhospitality of the people. In the 16 references in Scripture to the Genesis 19 account, there is not one support that the fire and brimstone which hailed from heaven came as the result of homosexual love.

Those persons who quickly quote Leviticus and that book's condemnation of men lying with men had best read the entire law and be amused at the variety of violations we all merrily incur daily. Those who pick and choose what they wish to quote should read Leviticus 11:9-12 the next time they sit down to lobster or New England clam chowder.

Jewish condemnation (death by stoning) of homosexuality and sodomy (anal intercourse) did not surface until after the Babylonian captivity. Until that time, there was no law against same-sex lovemaking. But the race of people that was small in size and threatened constantly by larger tribes and races began protecting itself by insisting that all sexual activity have procreation as its end.

Men could not lie with men because they wasted the seed of procreation — the only means of increasing the numbers of the Jewish people. There is, oddly enough, no law against women lying with women. But that may also reveal the Jewish attitude toward the importance of women.

It has also been suggested that the condemnation of sodomy — an act which can be and is performed by both heterosexual and homosexual couples — is the response of a degraded people to a practice which was used by their Babylonian captors as a visible sign of supremacy. Sodomy is used synonymously with homosexuality under the supposition that all homosexuals engage in anal intercourse. The supposition is false.

Homosexual prostitution, the third source of Jewish condemnation, was so closely identified with idolatry (Ashtoreth and Baal) in the Jewish mind that the terms were often interchangeable — condemnation of one was condemnation of the other — much like the late Senator McCarthy's association of homosexuality and treason.

As a group of monotheists in a world dominated by polytheists, the Jews condemned anything associated with the worship of false gods. Into this culture was born Saul of Tarsus, a good Jew whose zeal for the Faith brought forth a new testament of beautiful writings, inspired by the teachings of the Messiah. But Paul's writings also reveal his Jewish bias in the areas of women and sex and his own personal "thorn in the flesh" hangups in others.

It is with the Pauline writings that Christians are most inconsistent. Few today will quote Paul when he advises men to cut their hair short and women to cover their heads and be subject to their husbands. Even the most dedicated celibate will water down Paul's incredible approach to marriage and sex.

But who holds back a single syllable when the man writes his condemnation of the homosexual? St. Paul is divinely inspired. Surely he speaks for God!

Without such Scriptural criticism, however, the church went forward, guided by Christ's beautiful message of love (a message which incidentally never mentions homosexuality) and burdened by a reactionary tradition of legalism, sexism and a contempt of the flesh.

The first formal legislation against the homosexual in the church (in which pederasts were denied last rites), according to John Lauritsen in his *Religious Roots of the Taboo on Homosexuality*, was enacted at the Council of Elvira in 300 A.D.

As with all other abuses, the sufferings began worldwide for the homosexual when Christianity was declared the state religion by Constantine in the early fourth century.

In 342 A.D., a decree imposed the death penalty for sodomy. In 390, Emperor Valentian initiated death by burning, in the tradition of Sodom and Gomorrah.

An edict of Theodosius banned all religions other than
Christianity. Loyalty to the state, according to Lauritsen,
demanded loyalty to the laws of the Faith, including the code
of sexual morality. Heresy equalled treason. Soon after,
homosexuality was seen as heresy, which in turn, was a trea-
sonous offense.

In 538, Justinian codified the Roman law and subsequently prescribed torture, mutilation, and castration for
homosexuals.

Justinian's *Novella 77* blames homosexuality for fam-
ines, earthquakes, and pestilences. Sodomites, as they were
called, were put to death, lest the entire city and its inhabi-
tants perish.

Justinian's *Novella 141* speaks of homosexuality as ". . .
such as have gone to decay through the abominable and
impious conduct deservedly hated by God."

The effect of Justinian's policies is summed up in *Phallos*
by Thorkil Vanggaard, who states:

"Thus what was originally an exclusively Jewish attitude
towards homosexuality and phallic symbolism had gained as-
cendancy over the whole Christian world. A true Christian
believer was marked out from then on by his unconditional
condemnation of everything homosexual. Correspondingly,
homosexual acts were regarded as unshakeable proof of
heterodoxy."

During the Dark Ages, homosexuals were punished by
the church with excommunication, denial of last rites, castration, torture, mutilation, death by burning, and burial in
unsanctified ground. Some church fathers, from fear of
"pollution," also insisted that the corpses be mutilated.

As the church began waging battle on heretics throughout Europe, slaughtering thousands under the sign of the
Cross, so too did it gleefully dispose of any living creature
who was suspected of being a homosexual. Heresy and
homosexuality were inseparable.

"During the Middle Ages, heretics were accused of un-
natural vice as a matter of course," writes Westermarck in

Origin and Development of Moral Ideas. "Indeed, so closely was sodomy associated with heresy that the same name was applied to both."

In the 13th century, St. Thomas Aquinas insisted "right reason declares the appointed end of sexual acts is procreation." In the tradition of his predecessor Augustine, Aquinas viewed homosexuality as an evil because the acts could not result in procreation. They were, therefore, *peccata contra naturam* (sins against nature).

Aquinas even went so far as to assert that masturbation was more evil than forcible rape and incest, reasoning that rape and incest could result in blessed procreation. Masturbation, obviously, could not.

Sodomy, by the Middle Ages, was referred to as *peccatum illud horribile inter Christianos non nominandum* — the sin so horrible that it must not be mentioned in the presence of Christians. Those who question the influence of the church would do well to check the English criminal law where they will find the same wording used into the 19th century.

The term "faggot," a favorite term of opprobrium, owes its origin to the Roman Catholic Church. A faggot was a measure of sticks which were bundled together for burning . . . most often the incineration of a heretic.

From the Oxford English Dictionary comes the explanation, "With special reference to the practice of burning heretics alive, especially in phrase 'fire and faggot,' and to 'fry a faggot'; to be burned alive."

The Inquisition delighted in burning faggots. "Homosexuality in the Middle Ages," according to historian Henry Kamen, "was treated as the ultimate crime against morality, and the standard definitions of it refer to the 'abominable' or the 'unspeakable' crime. . . . The usual punishment was burning alive." (*The Spanish Inquisition.*)

When Protestants went their own way, most often leaving behind what they considered the evil thinking and practices of the Roman Church, they generally carried with them

the sexual code of condemnation. Henry VIII in England and
the Calvinists in Amsterdam continued the legacy of homosexual annihilation.

It wasn't until 1861 that the death penalty was removed
in England for sodomy. In Scotland it remained the practice
until 1889. Homosexuals in Nazi Germany were shot without
trial or sent by the thousands to extermination in Hitler's
infamous concentration camps.

This all took place proudly under the banner of the
Judeo-Christian ethic. No anti-homosexual taboo existed in
China, Japan, India, the Arab countries or pre-Columbian
America.

Even today, in 1975, homosexual activity is a punishable
"offense" in nearly every state in this country. In some states
the punishment is life imprisonment. In others, homosexuals
are sent to state hospitals where they are given shock treatment and vomiting-inducing chemicals, as in *A Clockwork
Orange*, to convert their behavior to a more acceptable
pattern of sexual response. The therapy is overwhelmingly
unsuccessful and psychologically destructive, but it continues, all the same.

What hurts the Catholic homosexual who loves the
church and who tries to live a life based on Christ's selfless
law of love, is that the unchallenged champion of oppression
against the gay community is still the Roman Catholic
Church.

The main headline of the May 24, 1974 *New York Times*
reads, "Council, by 22-19, Defeats Bill on Homosexual Rights
. . . Opposition by Archdiocese Cited as Key Factor on
Vote."

"It was the opposition of the Roman Catholic
Archdiocese of New York," the *Times* article read, "that most
politicians cite as the key factor in the defeat of the measure
which would have banned discrimination in housing, jobs or
public accommodations because of 'sexual preference'."

The bill sought only to guarantee the homosexual the
right to live where he or she wanted to live and to work

where he or she wanted to work. The bill said nothing about the moral rightness or wrongness of being a homosexual.

In this post-Vatican II era the Roman Catholic Church has prided itself in the often late but strong defense of the oppressed. Blacks and Chicanos have a friend and ally in the Roman Catholic Church. Even women are beginning to make some headway in an institution as sexist as Hugh Hefner.

But with a group of people estimated to be 20 million strong in this country, a group which has one of the highest suicide rates among oppressed people, a group the *Wall Street Journal* refers to as our "last minority," the Roman Catholic Church leads the battle in Goliath fashion against even those who seek to remain faithful.

". . . within a few days, a front-page editorial in *The Catholic News*, the official newspaper of the New York Archdiocese, labeled the measure a threat to family life and urged its opposition," the *Times* reported.

"The church action prompted a torrent of mail and of opposition resolutions from neighborhood groups — veterans' posts, Holy Name Societies and civic organizations — that put the bill in trouble."

Similar action and opposition was equally successful in Worcester, Massachusetts, and Philadelphia. In both cities, the church sought to save the people from "pollution."

But the oppression of gays is not always blatant enough to make headlines. Most every day Catholic homosexuals feel far more subtle forms of blind, ignorant persecution.

The homosexual penitent, for instance, is advised, through the direction of the National Conference of Catholic Bishops, that celibacy is his or her calling. All homosexuals by virtue of their orientation (for which they had no choice) are called to a life of sexual abstinence in the eyes of the church.

"I haven't been to the sacraments in 15 years," writes one man. "How do you reconcile your sexuality with your Faith? Do you receive Communion?" "My confessor tells me that I am living in sin," confides another. "He insists that I report to him every Saturday."

"My friend is a convert to the Faith. He is gay but because he wants to be a priest he has announced that he hates
homosexuals. What do I do for him?"

"I am a nun. I have loved another nun for 12 years. Is
there anything you can say to us that will help us to understand how God views us?"

Perhaps the most disturbing question came from a
friend, a former Franciscan, who, after sharing in the Liturgy
took me aside and asked in all sincerity, "Brian, do you think
we are really going to hell?"

Living in a secret world for as long as they can remember, the homosexuals are forced to be islands unto themselves. Childish fears and fantasies and a million unanswered
questions are kept penned up within. Communication is impossible; sharing too threatening.

Where, for instance, does the male homosexual turn
when at age 14 he is more attracted to the foldout in *Playgirl*
than he is to the one in *Playboy*?

Whom does he confide in at age 18 after having had his
first sexual encounter with another human being?

How does a man explain that he has "fallen in love" with
another man to heterosexual friends and relatives? Worse
yet, where and to whom does he go when he has lost his first
love and aches inside as he has never ached before?

His Mom and Dad? Sister Mary? Brother Duffy? Msgr.
McPhillips? His doctor? His friends?

The horror stories of gay men and women are consistent
in revealing the same treatment over and over again when
they dared to share with a "straight" their homosexuality.

One young man was called outside the confessional,
where he was promptly "decked" by the priest-confessor.
Another tells of how the priest went to the parents of his
friend and insisted their son not be allowed to continue the
friendship.

Some parents have been known to order their children
out of the house until their "orientation changes." Others

smile sympathetically as they wildly leaf through the phone book looking desperately for a psychiatrist.

Upon sharing his orientation with his charismatic prayer group, one Detroit gay was told to either submit himself to the "healing power" of the group or never come back. "Praise the Lord, we love you brother, but God says in Genesis 19 . . ."

For that reason, the phone calls and letters pour in.

"I am 15. I read about you in the paper and I wondered if maybe you could introduce me to someone. I'm really lonely."

"I'm married . . . have been for 12 years. I have a son, but I'm not happy. I'm not gay if I'm married, right? Then why do I feel the way I do?"

"I'm 84 and for the majority of my life I have been a prisoner of fear. I pray that what you are doing will free others who follow to live freely."

Live freely? Ultimately it is the decision of the individual. And it is called "coming out" in the gay community. It means accepting one's homosexuality and sharing that orientation with family, friends and working cohorts. The degree to which the homosexual can do that determines the degree of his or her freedom. But always there is a price. The greater the freedom, the greater the price.

My freedom began only after 25 years of hiding, of keeping my secret, of being what others thought I ought to be.

"Who are you taking to the prom, Brian?" "I saw Sarah Murphy's mother the other day. She said Sarah's home. Why don't you ask her out?" "Hey, McNaught, how many broads have you had?" "That one ought to be married. He'd make a fine father."

The nightmare ended in a bottle of paint thinner. With tears flowing freely in the Emergency Room at St. Joe's Hospital — a tube down my throat pumping out my stomach — I promised myself that I would never again live for the whims and expectations of other human beings.

This promise was not an easy one for me. After the local

newspaper identified me as a homosexual and as president of
the local chapter of Dignity — a national organization of gay
Catholics — my column in a diocesan newspaper, in which I
had previously defended Christian gay love, was dropped.
The editors said they eliminated my column because of
space limitations, though I find it difficult to believe this was
the real reason.

Later I began a public fast and was subsequently fired as
a staff writer for the diocesan newspaper. The editors claimed
I had terminated my own contract.

Until the headlines about my case hit the local press last
year, homosexuality was not something commonly discussed
in the chancery. As one bishop confessed to me, "I have read
more about homosexuality in the last week than I have in my
entire ministry."

So while the incident was a personal hardship for me,
there were some ensuing events which, I think, are a sign of
hope for both gay Catholics and the church. It might be helpful to look at these.

After my column was dropped, a conference of gay
Catholic activists and sympathizers was organized. It was to
be a study weekend which included a Mass of solidarity and a
silent, peaceful march to the chancery "to give visible witness
to the belief that the love of God extends to all persons,
regardless of sexual orientation, guaranteeing for them the
right to the pursuit of happiness and the Christian ideal."

Perhaps because the conference was opposed by the
archbishop (who described gay people in a letter as those
with "arrested sexual development") or perhaps because
heterosexual Catholics can't afford to be mistaken as gay, the
turnout was smaller than the organizers had hoped for. But
the clergy and religious who did attend were an important
source of hope to the assembled community.

One of them, veteran humanitarian Msgr. Clement
Kern, said, "All of us, gay and straight alike, have come here
today to affirm ourselves before God in faith; to accept ourselves without regrets or self-pity; and to seek a good and full

life in keeping with our potential for growth and God's call. "We especially regret the misconceptions, taboos, biases and fears which are directed at our gay brothers and sisters. If growing to sexual maturity is difficult for straight people, the constant barrage of ridicule, ignorance and condemnation which falls on gay people demands that their efforts at growth be almost superhuman."

And yet there are more homosexuals than most people think, and they tend to be as well-adjusted, productive, and as interested in pursuing traditional ideals as any group. Homosexuality is not chosen. It, like heterosexuality, is the result of a variety of conditions, probably both psychological and physical. Many homosexuals are as intent upon settling down with one person as are heterosexuals. And statistically, their relationships last as long.

The American Psychiatric Association virtually admitted that homosexuality is not a disease when it voted unanimously in 1973 to remove homosexuality from the diagnostic and statistical manual of psychiatric disorders.

Unfortunately, the myths and stereotypes about homosexuals rather than the new attitude of the American Psychiatric Association seem to be more characteristic of the church. So it was the task of the weekend conference to find a way to communicate with an institution which seemed to refuse to listen. Does one picket? Write a letter to the editor? Ask for an audience with the bishop?

For me, the only authentic, nonviolent, Christian method was a prayerful fast. No food. No drink. Scripturally, it seemed a sound vehicle of communication, of calling attention to an evil, of making reparation for what I saw as a grave sin on the part of the church.

"As a man who loves his church and as a gay who loves his gay brothers and sisters," my fast statement said, "I am in daily torment.

"Fully believing in the mission of my church to bring all persons into the Divine Presence through the example of the selfless love of Jesus, I embrace my Faith and the community of believers and dedicate myself to that goal.

"Fully sharing in the normal sexual orientation of my gay brothers and sisters, I am led by the same natural human drives for creative loving union with a person of my choosing, regardless of gender.

"But my love for my church and my love for my gay brothers and sisters are in conflict. My church does not love my gay brothers and sisters. My church unscrupulously persecutes them. This I can no longer tolerate spiritually, physically, or emotionally."

My fast lasted 24 days, 17 of which were on water. It took those 24 days, 24 pounds, and mostly sleepless nights, before the church responded.

The two auxiliary bishops who were in town at the time delivered a letter to us:

"From the outset, let us say that we respect the motives behind your fast and the sincerity of your efforts. . . .

"The gift of sexuality deserves deeper understanding and appreciation than has often been given in our society and in our church. Some efforts toward continuing education in this regard have been made. A priests' workshop on sexuality is being planned for the near future and we, on our part, will support it fully. We will urge that special attention be given to the question of homosexuality. . . .

"While the Catholic Church, in view of its moral teaching, cannot endorse or condone overt homosexual acts, we have a serious obligation to root out structures and attitudes that discriminate against the homosexual as a person. We will exert our leadership in behalf of this effort.

"We hope for your continued cooperation with us in trying to achieve this goal."

There were some who were disappointed with the letter and with my decision to end the fast. However, those of us who had dealt with the church in this and in other areas over the years knew that we had received more than met the eye.

Catholic gays want to stay within the church. As much as anyone else, they love their cultural heritage and the guiding challenge of the Faith. The Mass and the Sacraments and the Nicene Creed are as rich in meaning for the Catholic homosexual as they are for the Catholic heterosexual.

No one should have expected the bishops to issue a public statement reversing 2000 years of procreative theology. If such a reversal comes, it will begin with theologians. But the bishops pledged an effort at education, and where there is the pursuit of education there is the pursuit of truth.

Homosexuals cannot be hurt by truth. Only helped. ∎

Gay and Catholic
April 1979

Growing up gay and Catholic can be like living in Northern Ireland with a Catholic mother and a Protestant father. Loyalty to one seems to preclude loyalty to the other. Not only do gay Catholics receive a consistently clear message from the hierarchy of the Catholic community that their sexual orientation is "seriously disordered" but they also hear from the other front that maintaining Catholic ties "perpetuates the oppressor." While a decision between loyalties is frequently called for, there is no need to make a choice.

Traditional condemnation *by* the Church is based on a lack of understanding of homosexuality and upon an imposed understanding of human nature, justified by faulty interpretation of Scripture. Condemnation *of* the Church also reflects a limited understanding of the true meaning the Church has and can have in people's lives.

Theologians of the Roman Catholic Church in the United States take one of three basic positions on the morality of homosexuality. The traditional stand, as enunciated by the *Vatican Decree on Certain Questions Concerning Sexual Ethics*, insists that the basic purposes of sexual activity are procreation and expressions of mutuality (conjugal love). Insofar as homosexual love-making does not satisfy the requirement of procreation, it is a "misuse" of the genitals and therefore "disordered." (When confronted with the practice of blessing marriages of heterosexuals who are biologically incapable of procreating, the Church responds that there is at least the possibility of procreation, as with the story of Abraham and his wife Sarah, who though well beyond childbearing age , nonetheless, through the intervention of God, did conceive.)

The second position, adopted by theologians such as Charles Curran, considers homosexual behavior the lesser of two evils *if* the individuals involve themselves in a permanent relationship. This holds true only if they are unable to maintain a life of sexual abstinence. Richard McCormick uses the word "non-normative" when describing homosexual relationships but argues that he would bless such a union rather than encourage promiscuity by condemning the relationship.

The third position is that of Fr. John McNeill, the Jesuit who was silenced twice by Rome because of the popularity of his book *The Church and the Homosexual*, and by Gregory Baum. Both men place homosexual relationships on an equal par with heterosexual relationships by arguing that the individuals are being true to their nature.

In a book entitled *Human Sexuality*, a sexuality study group of the Catholic Theological Society of America drew heavy fire from the American Bishops for suggesting that not all homosexuality was morally wrong. Given the case of a "constitutional homosexual" (the individual who has made no choice of sexual orientation), the authors suggested that the same criteria would be applied to the homosexual's relationship as they present for the heterosexual. Is it "self-liberating, other-enriching, honest, faithful, life-serving and joyous"?

How then do gay Catholics reconcile themselves with these three positions? The answer depends upon what we mean by "Catholic." Some persons who call themselves Catholic mean they were baptized Catholic but have had no ties with the Church since they left home. Some Catholics, like myself, enjoy participation in the Church for a variety of reasons totally unrelated to the do's and don't's of man-made tradition. Others consider themselves Catholic because they go to Mass every Sunday, and while they don't especially like being Catholic, are afraid not to be for fear of eternal damnation. Michael, the pathetic character in "Boys in the Band," who rushed to midnight Mass at St. Malachy's after throwing his dehumanizing party, comes quickly to mind here.

There are Catholics who cannot act without justifying their actions with quotes from the Bible. There are Catholics who wait for direction from Rome or from the American Bishops or who place the total direction of their spiritual life in the hands of their local priest. In counseling Catholics who want to reconcile their homosexuality with their faith, therefore, it is not enough to share with them the processes which I went through in making my religion and my sexual orientation inseparable. Their age, their ethnic background, the number of years they spent in parochial schools, their knowledge of Scripture all contribute to make significant differences in the ease with which they will reconcile what seems to be the irreconcilable.

From my perspective, I made no choice in becoming a Catholic. Yet, I have no regrets. A Catholic background is not unlike a strong Jewish background insofar as it involves growing up with rules, rituals and cultural idiosyncrasies which separate you from many of your friends and provide common bonds with others, which become fun cocktail conversations at even the dullest parties. The Latin Mass, no meat on Fridays, the rosary, the May crownings, your new St. Joseph Missal, the nun's habits, being an Altar Boy and fainting from the incense, traditional rivalries with the athletic teams of the neighboring public schools, thoughts about entering the seminary or convent, holy cards, the "Decency Pledge" and a variety of other "typically Catholic" traditions are essential ingredients to my past which I share with other persons who grew up Catholic. And, as with my family, while I might privately be scandalized by some of the personalities or practices, I become incredibly uncomfortable when someone outside the "family" holds them up for ridicule.

From the spiritual vantage point, I have travelled the

same roads most persons with 16 years of parochial education have weathered. In grade school I was considered by the nuns to be a "prince of a boy." For several years I considered entering religious life and finally made a very fast visit (eight weeks) to a monastery of teaching brothers. At Marquette I went through the fashionable stage of being an "academic agnostic." Today, I find that my life has more meaning if centered around the existence of a God. Jesus holds particular significance as the individual who lived a perfect life of selflessness thereby liberating us from the legalism of religion and from the siren song of over-indulgence.

In the Roman Catholic Church I see millions of persons who shared my cultural background and who are therefore initially fun to be with; who like myself would not suffer torture at the hands of the "Communists" in defense of the Immaculate Conception, the Assumption or Papal Infallibility, but who all the same consider themselves an important part of the "Pilgrim People" stumbling through life in an attempt to incorporate the message of "Love God, Love Neighbor as you Love Self" into everyday transactions with grocery clerks, salespersons, parish priests, homophobic bishops and state representatives.

As Mass on Sunday can be more dehumanizing and alienating than staying at home, I frequently opt to celebrate and worship God alone or with friends in small community gatherings. I haven't been to confession since the priest at Marquette insisted masturbation was not sinful. If I encounter a period of spiritual-emotional isolation, I either sit down with my lover Ray and talk it through (fully respecting his personal, though uncelebrated spirituality) or I call a friend who happens to be a priest but is more importantly a person I respect.

How can I call myself Catholic given all of these apparent transgressions against the rules? I can call myself anything I choose and there is no priest, bishop or Pope who can tell me otherwise. Each person's life is a major gamble. People who choose not to believe in God are gambling that when they die there will be nothing. I gamble with my life that there will be. As a Catholic who is also gay I gamble that the official Church has misinterpreted the Will and Word of God. If I am wrong, then the Church tells me that I will pay the price. Yet, I cannot conceive of a God who would allow a person to live on this earth as an emotional cripple when that person need not make that choice. Likewise, when the Church publicly condemns me and leads campaigns to eliminate my civil rights, they too gamble. If they are wrong, which I am sure they are, they will encounter a God who will greet them with, "How could you do that to another human being in my name?"

As anyone who plays poker knows, it is next to insanity to gamble without a hand that can win. Gay Catholics sit at a table across from a person with far more chips to bet, with a reputation for being able to bluff countless others out of the game and with five cards which he insists are unbeatable: The Bible, Revelation, Tradition, the Keys to the Kingdom and Infallibility. Let's take a look at this "unbeatable" hand.

The Bible has been used since the first ink dried on Chapter One of Genesis to justify human actions. We have used it to condemn the Jews, maintain slaves, keep women in what we imagine to be their "place," condemn non-Catholics, condemn borrowing money from banks, condemn masturbation, condemn inoculation, justify the Crusades, and a variety of other practices or attitudes we weren't comfortable holding only ourselves but insisted that everyone else hold too. The Church cites Genesis, Leviticus and Letters of St. Paul to Romans and Corinthians and Timothy to build its case against homosexuality. However, a growing number of Scripture Scholars (whose writings the Church has cited in the past but now discredits) insist that all of those references to homosexuality have to be understood in the context in which they were written and that ultimately there is nothing in the Old or New Testament which speaks of behavior by "constitutional" homosexuals. Men of Science insist that until a few decades ago, it was always presumed that homosexuals were heterosexuals who were either emotional midgets or were deliberately deviating from their true orientation for the sake of "thrills." How then can the Bible have condemned something the writers of the Bible did not understand? Even given this argument, however, some persons believe that every word of the Bible is the word of God and that even if the writers didn't know about homosexuality, God did and planned their words for future reference. There is no arguing with these people except to point out to them the thousands of violations of the Bible which they commit in a single week. Anita Bryant, for instance, should know well the Bible's admonition against women speaking up to men! The first card of the "unbeatable" hand, therefore, shouldn't scare you out of the game.

Revelation is technically the revealing of divine truth through a variety of means. The Church has always insisted that it alone holds this card. While I personally have no doubts about the reality of revelation, I know for a fact that the Church is not the only recipient of divine truth. It has, for instance, been "revealed" to gay Catholics that God does not wish them to hate their homosexual orientation but to celebrate it in a manner consistent with the teachings of Jesus, i.e., to love selflessly. This knowledge has been put through a far more thorough "discernment" than the celibate teachers of the Church are able to engage in, for gay Catholics have had to live the truth and not merely talk about it. If there is such a thing as "truth," then living the truth must result in internal sensations of wholeness and joy. Such is my experience and the experience of thousands of other gay Catholics who have lived the truth. Gustavo Gutierrez, the Third World theologian who is captivating the minds of millions with his "Theology of Liberation" persuasively argues that the Gospel must have relevance to an individual's life in order to be acted upon. Put quite simply, you cannot tell starving people who live under a dictatorship, "Blessed are the Poor." Christianity, in that context, makes no sense. He instructs those who suffer persecution to examine the internal sources of their oppression and to interpret the Gospels in a way which makes sense. Revelation for Gutierrez does not come to us by way of an early Church scholar who "reasoned" out the Will of God but rather it comes to us from our own real experience of the world around and within us. As a person who has experienced levels of selfless love by way of homosexual lovemaking, the truth revealed insists that to abstain from that vehicle would be a living lie.

The third card is Tradition. The Church believes that anything that has survived its long history of scholarly probing and has withstood the test of time, must indeed be the Will of God. Yet, traditions change by the weight of new discovery. A case in point is the attitude toward women. The Church continues to cite tradition as a good reason for not ordaining women to the priesthood. In society, however, women are successfully challenging their "traditional" role. While the past held the lid on opportunities for women in the professional world, observers today insist it won't be long before a woman is elected Commander-in-Chief of the Armed Forces. When that happens, Rome will relinquish its tradition and ordain women to the priesthood, lest it appear totally irrelevant to people's lives. Likewise with the tradition which Rome insists condemns homosexual behavior. In his much-acclaimed book, *Christianity, Social Tolerance and Homosexuality*, Dr. John Boswell of Yale University shows that the Church has not always condemned homosexuality and that in fact, many of its early writers defended it against repressive laws. Obviously, the official Church will probably ignore Boswell's findings but it can't really rely on its tradition when it comes to a persistent denial of the moral neutrality of homosexuality any more than it could continue to condemn usury, Jews or condone slavery.

The Keys to the Kingdom is weak to begin with. It is based upon the recording of Christ's words to Peter that "Upon this Rock I will build my Church." His followers were told that whose sins they forgive are forgiven and whose sins they bind are bound. This power is handed down from Pope to bishop to priest through ordination, making each a representative of Jesus on earth. However, for a variety of reasons, this line of authority carries little ultimate weight in the lives of individual Catholics. To begin with, an essential teaching of the Church is that above all else, conscience must be the ultimate guide for behavior. No person can be told to do something or to refrain from doing something if that action is inconsistent with his or her own moral decision of conscience. The Church warns, however, that a conscience must be *developed* and that a means of developing your conscience is study of the Scriptures and the Revelation and Tradition of the Church. For the weak-minded, this provides a convenient "Catch 22." Do what your conscience tells you — but a truly developed conscience will tell you to do what we just told you to do. Those who do take their faith seriously have done the necessary homework to respond that while maintaining their allegiance to the Church, their consciences tell them they must disobey this particular instruction. According to statistics, over 80 percent of American Catholic couples have opted to use artificial means of birth control as a decision of conscience rather than follow the pronouncements of the Pope.

Contradicting a teaching of a person of spiritual authority in the Church is perhaps the toughest hurdle the gay Catholic has to conquer. Traditionally, Catholics with questions were always encouraged to "ask Father." While you never had the opportunity to "ask the Bishop," you did jump when the bishop spoke. And heaven help you if Rome made a pronouncement! The seriousness of this is best illustrated with reports we received of gay Catholics who committed suicide after the Vatican Decree on Sexuality seemed to close the door to any further debate on homosexuality. What must be remembered, however, is that the practice of "asking Father" developed when the clergy were the best-educated people in the world. Today most clergy would acknowledge that their training in the area of human sexuality was next to nil and that most bishops are in worse shape when it comes to any knowledge of homosexuality. Even priests recently ordained laugh about the fact that the section on sexuality was the only one of their studies which was written in Latin. When I went on my water fast in 1974 to protest the sins of the Church against gay people, I sent a gallon of water to the five Detroit bishops asking them to join me for a day. One responded positively and afterwards admitted that he read more on homosexuality in the 24 days that I fasted than he did in his entire career as a priest or bishop. Welcoming his honesty, I would have to admit major reservations about placing the Keys to my spiritual future in the hands of any individual who has no idea what a homosexual is.

There is not now, nor has there ever been a spiritual blanket of divine truth hanging over St. Peter's in Rome which prevents the Pope or those who surround him from making mistakes. The final card of the poker hand, Infallibility, was a man-made institution which was invented to keep protestors from becoming Protestants. It states that when the Pope speaks *ex cathedra* (from the chair) on matters of faith and morals that he will be free from error. From my perspective, it is sheer nonsense and the fact that it has rarely been used reflects perhaps a similar feeling by those in Rome. The Pope has made mistakes throughout the history of the Church, as have bishops and priests. What the Church condemns today (Martin Luther), it embraces tomorrow. For that reason, there is no pronouncement which comes out of Rome, the bishop's office or from the pulpit which should prompt any person to fully believe that he or she is "seriously disordered" or condemned to hell.

Now that we have called the bluff of the "pat hand," what cards do we hold? To begin with, any person who believes in God and believes that Jesus was the perfection of humanity so much so that he is the Son of God, and who attempts to live his or her life based upon the basic message of selfless love, approaches the poker table with an unbeatable

card, for there is no gamble involved there. Likewise, if we
have attempted to discern the externals of being a Catholic
from the essential ingredients which have been carried
through the ages by tradition (a thirst for justice, an ability to
forgive, an awareness of the Kingdom within) then our status
as Catholics cannot be undercut. If we have listened to the
voice within and have not been exploitative in our celebration of our homosexual orientation, then the pot is clearly
ours.

Lest anyone be confused, I love the Church. While I find
no meaning in Infallibility or the Immaculate Conception in
my life and while obligatory Sunday Mass has not created the
sense of community for me that it was designed to create, I
find no need to rid them of meaning in other persons' lives.
While I am contemptuous of authority which bases its power
over me on a magical formula, I believe in the potential
authority and power of the priesthood if it is exercised by
individuals who are called forth by the community to lead
with consent and who fully realize that they are being called
to serve and not to be served and feared. The Roman Catholic Church for me is not only an essential aspect of who I
am, given my 30 years at its breast, but more importantly, I
see it with adult eyes as a potentially powerful vehicle for
transforming the face of the earth into a Kingdom where love
replaces fear and hatred, and sharing eliminates want.

Gay Catholics are essential to the future of the Church.
We are a test which strikes at the very nerve of Christianity.
As society's modern "lepers," we are a constant indictment of
the lack of faith commitment of those who claim to be keeping all of the rules but who are unable to reach out in love as
they know they must. Our presence forces the decision
between being a Church of the People of God and a Church
of comfortable status.

Likewise, the unique beauty which the rivers of trial
have deposited with us provides us with a vision to be shared
with those whose eyes are scaled with contentment. The commitment to the Faith which gay Catholics personify by our

determination to sit through a service which condemns homosexuality (not unlike staying at a party throughout which you are the constant butt of the host's humor); to pray with brothers and sisters who would hold back the kiss of peace if they knew we were gay; to proudly announce our religious affiliation when the leaders of our Church have condemned us to hell, is a persecution for the Faith which most Catholics have only read about in the *Lives of the Saints*. When the work of the Spirit is completed and gay Catholics are liberated from the fear and hatred of the non-gay world, we will be celebrated.

Therefore, when we encounter representatives of the "official" Church who would have us believe God hates practicing homosexuals, it is important to convey by words and by actions the basic strength and pride that gay Catholics share. I make sure that the priest or bishop I encounter is made instantly comfortable with his fear of me by assuring him that I understand why he feels the way he does and am most willing to help him liberate himself from his un-Christian sentiments. We are making great strides forward. The hierarchy of the Church is more and more divided on the issue. While 10 years ago the subject of homosexuality was too embarrassing to discuss, today there are many bishops who have made strong public statements in support of full civil rights for gay men and women. There are even a few bishops who will privately confide that they find nothing morally wrong with homosexuality in a love relationship. Likewise, theologians and other educators are spending a great deal of time studying the subject and many have changed their positions because of their encounters with happy and healthy gay Catholics. While the thinking of the hierarchy and theologians does not affect me personally, I do rejoice in their change in attitude, for it will make it that much easier for the generations of gays who follow us to grow up feeling good about who they are. As with all movements toward the Kingdom, everything will come to pass. It is merely a matter of patience and perseverance.

As for those gay persons who are as vile in their attacks on our religious affiliation as some religionists are with our sexual orientation, it is important to remember that many of these persons are lashing out in anger. Most of them will identify themselves as "former Catholics," and for some reason they seem disturbed that not everyone hates the Church as much as they do. Patience, again, is required in explaining why the Church continues to hold meaning for you and also in helping the other discover why his or her feelings run so deeply. Such anger and bitterness are always more confining than liberating.

If gay Catholics play their cards right they can enjoy the riches of both their faith and their sexual orientation, which when combined and fully integrated are priceless. Both are essential to my life and as such, no one will be allowed to bluff me out of the game.   ∎

But Do You
Love the Church?

Winter 1980

The wrinkled brow across the breakfast table belonged to a
well-to-do Catholic who had, from time to time, financially
supported my efforts for reconciliation with the Church in
the past and was now listening to me wrestle with defeat.

As an admirer and previous backer of Boston street
priest Paul Shanley, my friend came to town to talk with us
about the national retreat house we were promoting for
lesbians, gay men and their families. Prior to that meeting, he
and I sat together, sipped Sanka and exchanged family and
Church news.

The night before he had dined with his bishop; the
Saturday prior he had donned overalls to paint a Catholic
home he had helped build for unwed mothers. Diligently
spiritual and delightfully simple, he loves his Church — our
Church. He cherishes his parochial education and laments
that his daughters no longer find Mass meaningful. His
charitable concerns range from being frequent honorary
director of diocesan fund-raising to secretly seeking funds to
help alcoholic bishops and clergy. As long as it is for the
Church and for people who seek to be part of the Church, it
commands his attention. For that reason, he was greatly dis-
tressed as I talked of my work as a gay Catholic as being "a
battle with despair."

Earlier, we had shared our major disappointment with
the Pope, with the treatment of Hans Kung and Bill Callahan
and with the seeming capitulation of the Dutch hierarchy.
Sensing his loyalty didn't suggest blindness, I began to build
my case for frustration. I told him the horror stories of
seminary witch hunts, about murdered gay clergy and religious and about the hypocrisy of closeted bishops. I mocked

the Vatican "Catch 22" position that homosexuals are incapable of embracing celibacy but must be celibate. I shared with him the intense bitterness of former Catholics who now "hate God" because the clergy have taught them God hates them. I recalled the telephone conversation I had with an anonymous medical student who desperately sought to speak with a sympathetic priest before he died of an overdose and how we couldn't find one available. ("What happened to him? I don't know. He hung up.") Because I knew he cared, I opened the dam and let gush forth my personal pain, anger and discouragement and that of my gay Christian friends.

"But you still love the Church, don't you?" he asked with eyes stretched open and eyebrows cocked expectantly.

For years the answer has been prompt, though not always easy. "Of course I love the Church," I would respond. "The Church is the people who seek to live the Gospel. I love the Gospel. I love the people. You and I are being used by the Spirit to renew the Church."

My heart ached with anxiety. My facial muscles quivered in confusion. He had asked the question I didn't want asked at that moment. Maybe next month; maybe next week; maybe even tomorrow, but not today. Today I am afraid of my response. Today I feel like the son of a highly-respected community leader who secretly beats her child. Today my pain is stronger than my devotion. Today I can't find the words to defend my parent against the curses of the neighbors and relatives who know. Today I fear I will stand rigid and scream "I hate the Church! I hate it! I hate it!"

But I didn't stand before my friend and scream. I sat paralyzed by guilt. I was immobilized by a secret sense of failure. I smiled weakly. It was enough of a "yes" to get by on. Sometimes, that's all I have.

There was a time, I explained, when I drew some strength from imagining myself watching the Pope, the bishops and certain pompous members of the clergy being confronted by God on the Final Day with all of the physical and spiritual anguish they caused lesbians, gay men and their families; confronted, like Hitler, with the wailing of homosexuals for all eternity. Today, my theology has changed, leaving me without the satisfaction of knowing I will watch the mighty fall.

"Gee," he said, hoping to brighten things up a bit, "I'm kind of banking on a heaven and hell and on encountering a God who will grant me eternal reward for bringing one person to the Church. That's what I've always been told," he said. "All you had to do to be saved was bring one soul back to the Church."

"And I'm afraid," I replied, "that my bringing one gay person back to the Church where I know he or she will be brutalized might be my ticket to your 'hell'."

A Trappist monk friend of mine suggests that I should have stood and screamed "I hate the Church." When I finished with that, he said, I "should stand and scream 'I hate God! I hate God!' " Until that happens, he said, I will have a child-parent relationship to both my Church and my God.

"There are three major crises in our lives," he said. "The first is when we discover our father isn't perfect. The second is when we discover the Church isn't holy. The third is when we realize Jesus isn't a magician. Until we enter these crises, we can't know the meaning of true love or true faith."

Long ago, I discovered my father's flaws and hated him for them. Now we are friends. The Jesuits were quick to make clear to me the fragile qualities of the traditional Jesus image and after feeling angry for being tricked, I can now love him as a brother. The Church, however, has a greater hold on me than either my father or Jesus. The Church has demanded total love and complete obedience. While my father and Jesus called me to adulthood, the Church has shielded me from reality, discouraged me from growing, forbidden me to be myself.

Gay Christians must admit their hatred of the Church before they can approach the Church as adults. Until we are able to stand rigid and scream out our anger, we will continue to be children who clamor for love and acceptance and who throw tantrums when we don't get it. Until we are able to believe that we are the Church, we will continue to bore adult Christians with our adolescent stories of what the bishop did to his priest secretary.

"But do you still love the Church?"

Not yet. I'm not finished being angry.   ■

Duplicity
Summer 1979

A letter arrived a few days ago from "the large Episcopalian who brought his own lunch" to a recent speaking engagement of mine in Miami. "I am writing to you," he said, "to share some sadness and some anger. . . . A friend of mine was murdered last week.

"He was a very closeted gay priest, vicar of a small mission. . . . He had been there eight years and was deeply loved by his congregation. The church secretary found his nude body, hands tied behind his back; his head had been beaten with a hammer.

"There are speculations about a young drifter who was taken in by the vicar and of course gossip about what may have happened. Whatever did happen may never be known, but what has disturbed me almost as much about his death is the way people have been reacting to it."

The letter then described an incredible conspiracy of silence by his friends, gay and straight, and by the local church. I say "incredible" but it wasn't at all. Undoubtedly, it was the fear of such a predictable reaction of raised eyebrows, deep sighs and silence which forced the vicar to remain in the closet in the first place. It was the fear of public scorn which prompted him to take foolish chances with a disturbed drifter so that he might know some warmth of human intimacy, no matter how limited. Surely it was the sinfully-distorted image of homosexuality, prompted by ignorance and perpetuated by silence, which filled the head of whoever it was who so mercilessly murdered the priest.

Since receiving the letter, I have agonized over my own role in the death of the vicar. Am I silent at times when my voice would help eliminate the kind of self-hate which prompts people to seek comfort in dangerous settings? Am I too polite in my political stance with the Church? Two events within the week intensified the emotional and spiritual wrestling match. The Boston media ran the story of a Catholic brother, studying for the priesthood, whose throat was slashed from ear to ear and who was stabbed in the back, chest and hand. A closeted homosexual, he too sought human contact, drove in from out of state (to protect himself), picked up a stranger, performed sexually and was murdered. He was found outside the motel room (a half-hour after registering under a phony name) when other guests were awakened by his screams. More raised eyebrows, deep sighs and silence.

About the same time the Episcopal vicar was buried, another funeral of an ordained Christian minister, also a closeted homosexual, was taking place up north. There were no raised eyebrows or deep sighs at this man's wake. He was considered a great priest, a Prince of the Church, a leading defender of the faith. Nor was there silence. His life prompted long and enthusiastic testimonies. Besides, none of his many hundreds of mourners knew he was a homosexual.

There is a direct correlation between the lives, deaths and funerals of these three men beyond the fact that all three were active homosexuals, ordained Christian ministers (or an aspirant) and fearfully silent about their sexual orientation. There is a connection between the mute consent of the respected bishop when his brother bishops publicly condemned homosexuality as a serious disorder and the violent deaths of the vicar and the brother; a corollary between the image of heterosexual propriety which all three, like thousands of other homosexual clergy, attempted to maintain and the self-righteous viciousness of the two murders.

I have known for some time that the celebrated bishop, like various other members of the hierarchy, was a homosexual and for that reason feel that I too share in the death of the vicar and the brother. Perhaps if I and others had not protected the bishop, the Church might have more aggressively tackled the issue and set about the task of educating its people. Perhaps if we privately confronted those bishops who publicly oppose civil rights for gays, legislation would finally pass and attitudes would change. Perhaps we gay Christians share the responsibility for our oppression.

The emphasis is on the word "perhaps." For that reason my days are filled with prayers for guidance, long discussions with other gay Christians and strategy debates with other activists. The other side of the question became clear to me on a TV talk show five years ago. Jeannine Gramick and I were debating Kenneth Baker, an ultra-conservative Jesuit theologian who condemned me to hell. When I suggested there was a higher percentage of homosexuality in the clergy than in the general population and that included members of the hierarchy, Baker turned beet red. "Name one!" he snapped. "Name just one!" "No," I said, "were I to mention names, you would try to do the same thing to those men that the Church in Detroit has done to me."

When I began working at the diocesan newspaper nine years ago, I became privy to information flowing through the Catholic grapevine — that network of journalists, priests, religious and middle-management laity whose loose lips have never sunk a holy vessel but whose firsthand tidbits do make life as a Church member much more interesting. For the last several years, most of the data to reach my ears has been about "who is and who isn't" homosexual among the clergy. Throughout this time, most especially when I was working with Dignity National, I wrestled with myself and with other gay Christians about the ethics involved in our political struggle. Should we be confronting the churches with the information; with the hypocrisy of their position? The debate became most intense on those occasions when seminarians were expelled by closeted rectors, when official documents were released and when certain bishops announced they would "go to jail" rather than hire a homosexual.

Yet, always we deferred. It would be dirty politics, we thought. It's slander. What if we're wrong? It isn't fair to the individual. We had better keep our noses clean if we hope to have future dialogues with the hierarchy.

In 1976, Richard Ginder, the highly controversial Pittsburgh priest who authored *Binding With Briars — Sex and Sin in the Catholic Church*, put us to the test and, in retrospect, I fear we failed. Appearing on the Phil Donahue Show, Ginder identified himself as a homosexual, suggesting that one in three priests was homosexual and challenged the Church's teaching on various areas of human sexuality. The response of the Church was to remove Fr. Ginder's faculties. The Director of the Delaware Valley Office for Television and Radio called Ginder's remarks "scandalous and irresponsible." In response to Ginder's allegation about the number of homosexual clergy, the same diocesan official, Fr. Leo McKenzie, said, "Unsubstantiated and unjustified charges do irreparable harm to the work and reputations of thousands of virtuous and dedicated priests." (Fr. McKenzie, you will recall, was just arrested in the gay district of New Orleans for propositioning a male vice squad officer in a porno bookstore.)

Fighting for his faculties, Fr. Ginder wrote a remarkably audacious letter to Bishop Vincent Leonard, Ordinary of the diocese, in which he pleaded: "But why the uproar? Is it because the *vulgus* somehow consider the very condition of homosexuality a personal disgrace, and stubbornly refuse to accept the notion of a continent homosexual? They will contemplate the concept of homosexuality so long as it remains remote from them as in historical personages . . .

"When the viewer is abruptly confronted with the Roman Catholic priest, the very pillar of propriety and examplar of respectability in his own community, happily proclaiming himself homosexual, albeit continent, that viewer is immediately subject to an emotional conflict that is all but unendurable.

"And this I intended. It is time for the public to grow up and face the truth that the estimated 15-20 million homosexuals in America constitute a cross-cut through every level of society from top to bottom. I meant to shake them up and set them thinking. Just off-hand, I could name at least 10 of our

Pittsburgh priests who are homosexual and I dare say you could name three times as many. Of the Hierarchy . . ." At this point, Ginder broke the polite silence by naming bishops, living and dead, who he said "were well known for years in the gay underground as homosexuals, practicing or otherwise, with clear proof from lawyers and physicians still living."

It has been nearly four years since Ginder sent that letter to Bishop Leonard and 32 others, including Phil Donahue, Andrew Greeley, six American cardinals, the Apostolic Delegate and the officers of Dignity. We all, for one reason or another, greeted the letter similarly — with raised eyebrows and deep sighs. Perhaps worst of all, we greeted it with silence.

Ginder was being reckless, we thought. He won't get away with it. We've worked too hard to build a reputation of respect. Better put some distance between him and us. He's a political liability.

Richard Ginder might well have been a political liability at the time. He had been arrested six years prior on several charges of sodomy with adolescents. Yet, he was correct when he said the American public needed to be shaken up to "get them thinking." He confronted the Church with its hypocrisy and for so doing was publicly attacked by a closeted Church official. He sent out a call for help and was politely denied assistance by those of us who claimed to be the official channel of communication between homosexuals and their Church.

Perhaps if we had fought the suspension of Ginder's faculties by clamoring in his behalf, we might have lost our reputation for politeness but gained some ground in the battle against complicity. Maybe if we had put our good name and reputation on the line with Richard we could have built a powerful political force among gay Christians which would make Church leaders think twice before they dare to remove people like Fr. Paul Shanley from his ministry to sexual minorities; forbid retreats for gay women religious and remove qualified lesbians from executive posts merely for being gay.

It might even be true that if we had the fortitude back then to support the effort to confront the Church with the high number of homosexuals among its spiritual leaders, the bishop would possibly have had fewer mourners and testimonies but the Episcopal priest and the Catholic brother would be alive today, loving themselves as God intended.

Obviously, I'm still wrestling with it. I hope others are too. ∎

The Pope's Visit
September 1979

Some Catholic observers are suggesting there will be a major increase in the number of young men who decide to enter the priesthood and in the number of people attending regular Sunday worship services because of the Pope's visit to the United States. I predict there will also be a rise in guilt among a number of gay Christians and even an escalation in the number of lesbians and gay men who attempt to live their lives without sexual expression.

Some people will be shocked by that assessment, just as they are flabbergasted to read about the number of homosexuals who desperately seek out the help of people like Anita Bryant and Kent Philpott, "Born Again" Christians who wish to help us terminate our sexual activity in exchange for a sense of belonging.

We don't need government reports to tell us how depressed the American people are. We can sense the helplessness and hopelessness in our own homes. Nor do I need to remind myself about the sense of despair experienced by large numbers of lesbians and gay men who struggle against the odds to feel good about themselves.

In a world dominated by cynicism and in a ghetto permeated with self-hate, many gay men and lesbians I have encountered find the struggle for self-affirmation, the battle for wholeness, almost too much to bear. For those who have been ostracized by family and friends, jilted by lovers and who find no refuge in their worshipping community, the siren song of Anita Bryant and Kent Philpott is a last hope; a final step.

Anita and Kent tell us they love us. They tell us they want us to meet Jesus whose love is a soothing balm for the wounds which riddle our bodies. They promise they won't try to make us heterosexuals. For some gay brothers and sisters, that promise of love is enough of an incentive; they will try anything.

While the music played by Bryant and Philpott is a funeral dirge to my ears, I did weep as I watched Pope John Paul II travel through the streets of Boston and celebrate Mass on the Common. Home, alone, in front of my television, I wept without shame as I saw a million of my neighbors cheering in the rain a man whose face of gentle strength and whose message of compassion has mesmerized the world. I wept because I hunger for hope, I wept because I too want my burdens lifted; because perhaps this man who has suffered so will caress me with his love and stand between me and my foes. I wept because I knew he wouldn't.

"Faced with problems and disappointments," the Pope told his audience, "many people will try to escape from their responsibility; escape in selfishness, escape in sexual pleasure . . ." To whom is he speaking, I wondered? Surely there are gay men and lesbians in that audience who want to believe in him as much as I do; brothers and sisters who ache for the embrace of acceptance and love. Will they think he is talking about them when he says "selfishness . . . sexual pleasure"? Will they lose ground in their struggle for self-love because the Church which oppresses them with formal decrees and blatant discrimination seems inseparable from this gentle and dynamic pilgrim of the Gospel? Will they walk home feeling that the cheers of the listening audience were cheers against them as much as they were for the Pope? I think some did because I struggled with it.

The message of the Gospel is one of salvation; it is a promise of love. It speaks most clearly to the oppressed. It says that we shall be comforted. It says that the greatest commandment of God is that we love ourselves. In loving ourselves we are enabled to love our neighbor despite all of the elements which separate us. By superseding ego, by loving self and loving neighbor selflessly, we love God.

Anita Bryant and Kent Philpott, and most "Born Again" Christians I have met, unknowingly pervert the message.

They're not evil people; they're ignorant people. They don't understand their own faith and they surely don't understand love.

Pope John Paul understands love. He understands his faith. His struggle against oppression enabled him to identify with the Gospel. However, he has neither written nor said anything which suggests to me he understands homosexuality. He is a wonderful man whose trans-world journeys are inspiring hope in millions of suffering brothers and sisters and prompting major discomfort with that element of the human family which is too comfortable. But until he educates himself in the field of human sexuality, until his scholarship embraces the findings of the majority of social scientists today, he too causes in me more a sense of rejection than a sense of hope with his promise of love.   ■

Forgiveness
February 1981

An Evangelical Christian theologian once told me that active homosexuals "who turn to the Bible for salvation are looking down the barrel of a shotgun." The Laws of God are clear, he insisted, and unflinching.

The man in question was one of many hundreds of thousands who rallied around Anita Bryant in 1977 and joined *Newsweek* magazine in declaring her "God's Crusader." As her husband Bob phrased it, Anita had "put on the armor of God." In her own words, she was a modern day Deborah.

Today, the former national symbol of the perfect Christian wife and mother is divorced, recovering from a dangerous duet with drugs and alcohol and angry about the "fundamentalists who have become so legalistic and letter-bound to the Bible." Undoubtedly, she too is considered by her former friends to be foolishly encouraging God's double-barreled wrath.

Yet, as reported in the December, 1980, issue of *Ladies Home Journal*, Anita Bryant believes "in the long run, God will vindicate me." And so do I.

Like Rep. Robert Bauman, (R-MD), who championed the fight against civil rights for homosexuals during the day and allegedly solicited sex in gay bars at night, Anita Bryant got caught between her own reality and the way she was taught things ought to be. She says that from the very beginning her marriage was a disaster, but she nonetheless wrote books, like *Mine Eyes Have Seen the Glory*, in which she told one million readers how happy she and Bob were in their nuclear Christian family. She wanted to have a happy marriage "so badly that I only shared the good parts."

By day she posed with her husband and children for pictures in front of their living room Altar and decried gay civil rights as a threat to the American family. At night she fought

bitterly with Bob, ridiculed him in front of friends, flirted
with strangers and massaged her guilt with Valium. "When
some people feel a total inadequacy in themselves, they feel
threatened and jealous," she told the *Journal*.

Anita Bryant's major turnabout on such questions as gay
civil rights and feminist issues hasn't received the attention it
deserves from the nation's media. Perhaps that is because the
airwaves are now jammed with the loud warnings of Anita's
former supporters — the politicized Born Again fundamentalists — that Ronald Reagan and the new Congress had
better listen to the Word of God and the Moral Majority and
stay on the far right on such issues as busing, welfare, the
ERA, civil rights and SALT II.

It's a shame because I believe Anita Bryant has been
called upon to deliver a message of major significance. It
seems to me that her conversion from celebrated intolerance
to a philosophy of "live and let live" is a clear indictment of
the self-righteous and a promise of forgiveness. It is a
warning not to take yourself too seriously or God's embracing love too lightly. It is an invitation to accept yourself as
flawed though intrinsically good and to look not into the
barrel of a shotgun but into the welcoming arms of affirmation.

"I never dreamed what I feared most could happen to
me," confided Anita. "But divorce is a part of life, you know,
and we all are imperfect." In her pain, Anita came to discover
that homosexuality is a part of life too, as are the concerns of
women. "As for gays, the church needs to be more loving,
unconditionally, and willing to see these people as human
beings, to minister to them and try to understand them," she
said.

While it isn't always true, I frequently find that I am
more comfortable with people who are outside of approba-
tion than those whose lives seem to mirror society and funda-
mental churches' ideals. Those who are able to lay claim to
their own pain, their uniqueness, their deviation from the
norm generally seem to share the same experience of a loving

God that I experience. They seem more able to go beyond the law and tradition and be in touch with the human experience. People who suffer aren't as prone to put other people in boxes, like "Divorced Catholic," "Homosexual," "Welfare Recipient," "Women's Libber." They tend more to ask questions than to shoot from the hip. They talk honestly about their own feelings and abhor hypocrisy.

Jesus abhorred hypocrisy. In fact, he spoke out against it more frequently and with more vehemence than on any other human conduct. Hypocrites, for him, were those persons who pretended to be something other than they were. Hypocrites were the law-givers and the law-quoters who denied their own experiences as flawed people.

Anita Bryant and Robert Bauman are two recent examples of individuals who publicly denied their private pain and puffed-up images of propriety to cover their flaws and receive social sanction. They became heroes to law-quoters and others who didn't trust God's embrace. Their charades caused more havoc in their own lives and in the lives of countless others who were scourged by their actions and their words, all in the name of God. "This is not my battle, it's God's battle," Anita told Dade County voters.

I knew the campaign against my civil rights was not God's battle, at least not my God's. Nor was it God's battle when people waved their Bibles in defiance of Charles Darwin or burned crosses on the lawns of Jews or beat up anti-war demonstrators or voted against the ordination of women. The God that I know isn't being talked about on Jerry Falwell's television show or in fundraising letters from Born Again groups which quote Corinthians to raise money against human rights. That used to be Anita Bryant's God but it doesn't seem to be any more.

"God says the wages of sin are death," she told *Playboy* magazine in 1978, "and one little sin brings on another...It just gets worse as it goes on. You go further and further down the drain and it just becomes so perverted and you get into alcohol and drugs and it's so rotten that many...end up committing suicide."

Back then she was talking about homosexuality. Two years later, she confided that her marriage was so bad she was taking heavy doses of pills and alcohol and one night would have committed suicide had she not thrown her pills down the drain the evening before. Two years later, she talks about a God I experienced after attempting suicide because my life didn't conform to the letter of the law.

"Fundamentalists have their heads in the sand," Anita now states. "The church is sick right now and I have to say I'm even part of that sickness... They thought they could get me under their thumb, that I had such a responsibility to my 'righteous-leader' image, they thought that I would stay in that marriage. Well, I just couldn't hack it."

Welcome to the human race, Anita. Welcome to the world of the socially-stigmatized, religiously-ostracized human outcasts with whom Jesus, to the astonishment of law quoters, preferred to walk.

For me, being an adult Christian is letting go of your fear of what the Church, the news media or the neighbors have to say about your life. It's a commitment to love yourself because of those things which make you different and to enable others to love their uniqueness. Being an adult Christian is a commitment to God that you will do your best to grow to your full potential, to embrace your humanity, to live life fully, to be a channel of encouragement and forgiveness in the world, to be honest, caring, involved and hopeful. It isn't easy being an adult Christian. It can be quite painful to be true to yourself.

"Of course, I know I'm going to hurt some more until the healing has time to work," says Anita. "But anyway, God loves me now right where I am." And so do I.   ∎

ONE FINAL NOTE

"You are right when you say opinions mean little," Siddhartha told the Buddha before striking out on his own to experience truth for himself. No one is more aware of how little meaning opinions have than the person who spends his or her life offering them. Opinions can get you in trouble with those who hear them, especially if they are embraced as a universal truth. Some opinions are repeated over and over again because they seem to be consistent with life as it is experienced. Other opinions change dramatically as life unfolds new mysteries and new truths. Some opinions are intended to disturb peace; others are intended to bring it. One of mine which has been repeated and which is intended to comfort is that I like being gay because it is an essential aspect of who I am, and I like who I am and what I am becoming.

I Like It
November 1978

The young medical student finally blurted out the question which had been gnawing at him. "Do you ever regret being gay?"

"No," I said with a growing smile. "Sometimes I regret being so totally identified with my sexual orientation, but I never regret being gay."

"Wouldn't you really rather be straight?" asked one Jewish talk show host. "Would you rather be Christian?" I asked.

"Think of all the hostility you face," commented one black woman. "Because of that, wouldn't you prefer being heterosexual?"

"Who's telling who about hostility?" I queried. "How much would it take you before you wished you were white?"

As supportive as they might become, many straight people have a lot of difficulty thinking of homosexuality as an intrinsic part of a person's psychological makeup. Even if they can be convinced that gay people didn't choose to be gay, they still need to hear us admit we would rather be like them.

I like being gay. I like knowing there is something very unique and even mysterious about me which separates me from most of the rest of the world. I like knowing that I share a special secret with a select group of men and women who lived before me and with those special few who will follow.

I like walking at life's edge as a pioneer; as an individual who must learn for himself the meaning of relationship, love of equals, sexuality and morality. Without the blessing of the Church and society, my life is one outrageous experiment after another. I like knowing that if I settle into a particular frame of thought, it is because I have found it appropriate and not because I was raised to believe that's the way things must be.

I like knowing that I can go anywhere in the world and meet someone who will smile that knowing smile which instantly says "Yes, I know; me too. Isn't it nice to not be alone? Hang in there." It is a twinkle and a smile which results not from being white or male or Catholic or American. It is a secret smile which only gay men and lesbians exchange.

I like exchanging that knowing smile with waiters in Galveston, flight attendants in Terra Haute, theater ushers in Detroit, salespeople in Boston and sunbathers in Sarasota. I like to give and receive those smiles at Mass, at lectures, in department stores, at the laundromat and on the street. I like the feeling I'm not alone.

I like believing the studies which indicate gay folk are generally smarter, more creative and more sensitive than non-gay folk. It makes me feel "chosen." I like knowing that a gay man's dinner party will usually be more elegant, that a gay-orchestrated religious service will usually be more artistic and that a gay disco will generally be more fun.

I like knowing that there is far less class division to be found at most gay parties. Janitors and lawyers and truck drivers and librarians are bound to unknowingly bump elbows and even likely to sit next to Lily Tomlin, Paul Lynde, or half of the Ice Follies.

I get a kick out of knowing that anti-gay people are probably wearing clothes designed by a gay person, living in a home decorated by a gay person, attending a play performed by a gay person and participating in a Sunday service celebrated by a gay person.

I laugh when I think of anti-gay men cheering gays on the football field and learning about other scores from a gay sportscaster. I especially love the thought of anti-gay Catholics praying to gay saints.

I like being gay for all of these and many more reasons. Primarily, though, I like being gay because it is an essential aspect of who I am . . . and I like myself.   ∎

About the Author

Brian McNaught is an award-winning freelance writer, a lecturer and a certified sex counselor. He has worked full time with the gay civil rights movement since 1974.

Upon receiving his journalism degree from Marquette University in 1970, Mr. McNaught began work as a conscientious objector at *The Michigan Catholic,* newspaper of the Archdiocese of Detroit. While there, he wrote an award-winning weekly column, became a popular host of a diocesan television program and was a frequent speaker at senior citizen group meetings, high school classes and Father-Son, Mother-Daughter Communion breakfasts.

In 1974, Mr. McNaught "came out" in the *Detroit News* as an affirmed homosexual. His column was immediately dropped by the newspaper. After a water fast in reparation of the Church's sins against gay men and women, which ended 24 days later when the local bishops pledged to work to educate the clergy about homosexuality, he was fired from his other responsibilities at the paper.

The founder of the Detroit chapter of Dignity, the organization of gay and concerned Catholics, Mr. McNaught served for a year and a half as national director of social action. During that time he represented and successfully lobbied for gay Catholics at the U.S. Bishops' 1976 bicentennial conference, "A Call to Action." He has edited two gay newspapers and was one of the three original directors of Exodus Center, an organization seeking to create a retreat facility for gay people and their families.

In 1976, Mr. McNaught received the Catholic Press Association's Journalism Award for Best Magazine Article of the Year. The article, "The Sad Dilemma of the Gay Catholic," appeared in the *U.S. Catholic* (August, 1975). Other religious publications to which he has contributed include the *National Catholic Reporter* and the *Witness,* a monthly magazine of the Episcopal Church for which he has served as guest editor. In 1979 he served as consultant to and is featured in the Guidance Associates filmstrip presentation, "The Hidden Minority: Homosexuality in Our Society." Brian McNaught's column, "A Disturbed Peace," has been run regularly by gay-oriented publications since 1974 and has appeared in newspapers and magazines published in Houston, Pittsburgh, Cleveland, Milwaukee, Detroit, Miami, Philadelphia, Boston, San Diego and Washington, D.C. Another piece, "Brian's Column," appears regularly in *Insight:*, the gay Christian quarterly. In addition to his work in periodicals, Mr. McNaught contributed the chapter on being "Gay and Catholic" to Betty Berzon and Robert Leighton's book *Positively Gay* (Celestial Arts, 1978). His work also appears in the college text, *Humanistic Psychology, A Source Book* (Prometheus Books, 1978), which includes his article, "Why Bother With Gay Rights?" from the September/October 1977 issue of *The Humanist* magazine.

In 1978 and 1979, Mr. McNaught was named one of the Outstanding Young Men of America. In 1979, he also received the Margaret Sanger Award from the Institute for Family Research and Education at Syracuse University for his contribution to the general public's understanding of homosexuality. He has spoken at over 20 colleges and universities and recently addressed the 1981 annual convention of the American Association of Sex Educators, Counselors and Therapists.

Mr. McNaught currently works out of his home in Gloucester, Massachusetts, which he shares with Ray Struble, his partner of ten years, their Irish Setter, Jeremy, and their canary, Bing Crosby.   ■